BIBLE CROSSWORDS

More Than 40 Crossword Puzzles

Edited by
Ellyn Sanna

BARBOUR BOOKS
An Imprint of Barbour Publishing, Inc.

© 2000 by Barbour Publishing, Inc.

ISBN 1-57748-671-4

All Scripture, unless otherwise noted, is taken from the King
James Version of the Bible.

Scripture quotations marked NKJV are taken from the New King
James Version, Copyright ©1979, 1980, 1982 by Thomas
Nelson, Inc. Used by permission. All rights reserved.

Published by Barbour Publishing, Inc., P.O. Box 719,
Uhrichsville, OH 44683 http://www.barbourbooks.com

Member of the
Evangelical Christian
Publishers Association

Printed in the United States of America.

BIBLE
CROSSWORDS

PUZZLE 1

Teri Grottke

ACROSS

1. "But whoso hath this____ good" (1 John 3:17)
6. Ratio of the weight of a given volume of a substance to that of an equal volume of another substance (abbr.)
8. Operatic solo
9. Mother of Hezekiah (2 Kings 18:2)
12. Kind; sort (pl.)
15. Gorged
17. Tall spar
18. Time frame? (abbr.)
19. O.T. book (abbr.)
20. Crush
22. Angered
27. Frequent follower of what or as
28. Good buy (colloq.)
29. Great Commission verb
30. Relative of corp.
31. Teacher
32. Near
33. Capital of Moab (Numbers 21:15)
34. Father of Heber (Luke 3:35)
35. Cried
37. Pile
39. "And he [Josiah] defiled ____ " (2 Kings 23:10)
42. Absalom rode one
45. ____ down
46. "False teachers. . .who. . . bring in ____ heresies" (2 Peter 2:1)
49. Noxious weed
52. Outside; outer (prefix)
53. Those not included in the clergy
55. Conjunction
56. Benign skin tumor
57. Greek letter
58. Engineering field (abbr.)

DOWN

1. "Before Abraham____, I am" (John 8:58)
2. Mouth (pl.)
3. Traditions
4. Father-in-law of Michal (1 Samuel 25:44)
5. What Lot did in the gate of Sodom
6. "____ called Zelotes" (Luke 6:15)
7. Mirror
10. Chem. symbol
11. Part of the psyche
13. Midwest state (abbr.)
14. State or Main (abbr.)
16. Preposition
19. Father of Mary's husband (Luke 3)
20. Minor prophet
21. Prior to this (arch.)
22. Type style (abbr.)
23. Father of Solomon's adversary (1 Kings 11:26)
24. Thing to hail
25. Land of Moses' birth

26. Kind of doctor (abbr.)
28. Spanish matron (abbr.)
32. One of the sons of Zophah (1 Chronicles 7:37)
34. "And all the women. . . brought that which they had ____" (Exodus 35:25)
35. Reporter's question
36. Chem. symbol
38. "I will not give thee of the land of the children of ____" (Deuteronomy 2:19)
40. Is in debt (arch.)
41. Favorite school subject, for some (abbr.)
43. ____ land
44. Son of Shobal (Gen. 36:23)

46. What washed Nebuchadnezzar in the wilderness for seven years (Daniel 4:23)
47. Hatchet
48. ____ service
50. Fish eggs
51. Before (poet.)
54. How one pronounces *ja*

PUZZLE 2

Teri Grottke

ACROSS

1. Son of Benjamin (Genesis 46:21)
4. Ruth's sister-in-law (Ruth 1:4)
9. Pronoun
11. Son of Zephaniah (Zechariah 6:14)
12. Wake
13. ____ what?
14. Son of Aram (Genesis 10:23)
15. Where the shewbread was
16. Skin
17. "____ thy cause with thy neighbour himself" (Proverbs 25:9)
19. Made useless
21. Family of exiles (Ezra 2:44)
22. The Great ____
23. More astute
24. Assistant to Ezra (Nehemiah 8:7)
27. Consume
28. Certain muscles, according to your personal trainer
30. Conjunction
31. Parched
34. City in Asher (1 Chronicles 6:75)
37. Grain mentioned in Isaiah 28:25
38. Exhaust
39. Are
40. "Come before his presence with ____ " (Psalm 100:2)
43. Give heed to
47. Esau's father-in-law (Genesis 26:34)
48. Miner's trove
49. Father of Jeroboam (1 Kings 11:26)
51. Solomon's great-grandson (1 Kings 15:8)
52. U.S. founder of Girl Scouts
53. Grate the teeth
54. Carve

DOWN

1. Second judge of Israel
2. He was given fifteen more years to live
3. Preposition
4. Daniel Webster, for one
5. What kings and sleepyheads wear
6. King of Assyria (1 Chronicles 5:26)
7. "Of the tribe of ____ were sealed twelve thousand" (Revelation 7:6)
8. Pronoun
9. Created
10. Regarded
13. Commandment mountain
15. Bible weed
16. " ____the Beth-elite" (1 Kings 16:34)
18. Exert or busy
20. Employ
23. Blanket or suit
24. Where Auntie Em lived (abbr.)
25. Also
26. Eight adults lived aboard this

28. Preposition
29. Near
32. Eve was made from one of Adam's
33. To Thomas, this was believing
34. Ancient Hebrew liquid measure
35. "The Pharisees began to ____ him vehemently" (Luke 11:53)
36. "Will the men of ____ deliver me and my men into the hand of Saul?" (1 Samuel 23:12)
38. One of the sons of Japheth (1 Chronicles 1:5)

40. One of the sons of Cush (1 Chronicles 1:9)
41. Proboscis
42. Chew
43. N.T. book (abbr.)
44. Mountain (comb. form)
45. "Behold, I make all things ____" (Revelation 21:5)
46. Lair
50. Chemical symbol (abbr.)

PUZZLE 3

Teri Grottke

ACROSS

1. 66 or 80, for example (abbr.)
4. Father of Ethan (1 Chronicles 6:44)
9. Laughing sound
11. Jether's son (1 Chronicles 7:38)
12. One of two
13. Preserve
14. Compass dir.
15. "Bread corn is bruised; . . . nor break it with the _____ of his cart" (Isaiah 28:28)
16. Ancient entrance
17. One of the families of the tribe of Benjamin (Numbers 26:39)
19. "They made their lives bitter. . .and in all _____ of service" (Exodus 1:14)
21. Certain vessels
22. _____ fried
23. Laziness
24. Achieve
27. Poetic contraction
28. April correspondent
30. Together with (prefix)
31. Wife of Joseph (Genesis 41:45)
34. Possessor
37. Commit larceny
38. Son of Roboam (Matthew 1:7)
39. Note on diatonic scale
40. Reluctant visitor to Saul in Damascus (Acts 9:10-17)
43. "Surely Moab shall be as Sodom, . . .even the _____ of nettles" (Zephaniah 2:9)
47. Biblical verb, KJV
48. Drum or drop
49. Son of Gad (Genesis 46:16)
51. Bind
52. She may be out to pasture
53. Identifies
54. Occurrence (arch.)

DOWN

1. Measles symptom
2. "For my soul is full of _____" (Psalm 88:3)
3. Apiece (abbr.)
4. Son of Levi (Genesis 46:11)
5. List components
6. Pronoun
7. Ship steering
8. European isle (abbr.)
9. Loathe
10. Unit of measure for manna
13. Father of Melchi (Luke 3:24)
15. "_____ meanest thou, O sleeper?" (Jonah 1:6)
16. Tiny winged insect
18. More destitute
20. Likely
23. Red or Dead
24. Simile component
25. "Out of whose womb came the _____? and the hoary frost of heaven" (Job 38:29)
26. Conjunction
28. Pronoun
29. With "factor," a group of antigens

32. Memo
33. Son of Gideoni (Numbers 1:11)
34. Minor prophet (abbr., var.)
35. "Who hath gathered the ____ in his fists?" (Proverbs 30:4)
36. Refuge for David, when first fleeing Saul (1 Samuel 19:18)
38. Hook
40. City of the tribe of Issachar (1 Chronicles 6:73)
41. Continent
42. Instruction manual word
43. Competition
44. Weather beaten

45. Before (poet.)
46. Gershwin
50. Linking verb

PUZZLE 4

Teri Grottke

ACROSS

1. "The earth shall _____ before them" (Joel 2:10)
6. Edify
11. Repast
12. Father of "mighty men" (1 Chronicles 11:34)
14. Pronoun
15. Fearful things
17. Look, see! (arch.)
18. Printer's measure
19. Bosc, Anjou, et al.
20. Name of two O.T. books (abbr.)
21. Date approx. 100 yrs. before Babylonian captivity, to Caesar
23. Age of Joshua when he died: one hundred _____
24. "Before Abraham _____, I am" (John 8:58)
25. Son of Judah (Genesis 38:11)
28. "Believe not every _____" (1 John 4:1)
31. "To meet the Lord in the _____" (1 Thessalonians 4:17)
32. Take advantage of
33. Gem in the fourth row of the ephod
36. Son of Pashur (Ezra 10:22)
39. Consumed
40. Owns
42. Article
43. Country part of the British Commonwealth, until 1961 (abbr.)
44. Sponsors
46. Linking verb
47. Conjunction
48. Fullness of this dwells bodily in Jesus
50. Number one?
51. "Doth not even _____ itself teach you" (1 Corinthians 11:14)
53. Son of Chislon (Numbers 34:21)
55. "A ram caught in a thicket by his _____" (Genesis 22:13)
56. Jobab king of _____ (Joshua 11:1)

DOWN

1. Extinguish
2. "What's _____?"
3. Suitable
4. Part of a castle
5. Maketh a mistake?
6. "Sow not among _____" (Jeremiah 4:3)
7. "Bringest certain strange things to our _____" (Acts 17:20)
8. Balaam's beast
9. Abbreviation preceding AKC winner
10. Son of Meraioth (Nehemiah 12:15)
11. What a dog often does

13. "Nor eat _____ grapes, or dried" (Numbers 6:3)
16. Feminine name
22. Put an end to
24. "They that are unlearned and unstable _____" (2 Peter 3:16)
26. Insolent talk
27. Linking verb
29. King of Assyria (2 Kings 15:19)
30. O.T. book abbr.)
33. Thessalonian Christian (Acts 17:5)
34. Wife of Jerahmeel (1 Chronicles 2:26)
35. Island Paul visited on his way to Tyre (Acts 21:1)
36. "Will he _____ thy riches?" (Job 36:19)
37. One of the children of Anak (Numbers 13:22)
38. His son was one of Solomon's twelve officers (1 Kings 4:10)
41. Residue
44. Symbol of power
45. Father of Heber (Luke 3:35)
48. King Ahaziah was wounded near here (2 Kings 9:27)
49. Accomplished
52. Preposition
54. Word in a command

PUZZLE 5

Teri Grottke

ACROSS

1. Returning exiles, the children of ____ (Ezra 2:44)
6. Standoffish
11. ____ of refuge
12. Mother of Samuel
14. "____ if!"
15. Encountered
17. Biblical pronoun
18. Latin abbr.
19. Made with yeast
23. Take a wrong turn
24. City where Isaac died (var., Genesis 35:27)
25. Physicians' group (abbr.)
26. Looked at
27. Greet
28. Gossips
30. Brother of Harnepher (1 Chronicles 7:36)
32. On the outside (prefix)
33. Son of Midian (Genesis 25:4)
35. O.T. minor prophet (abbr.)
38. Father of Azareel (Nehemiah 11:13)
40. More painful
42. Hearts, for one
43. Offering
46. Preposition
47. Hospital inits.
48. King Og's kingdom (Numbers 21)
49. Pronoun
50. Aka Belteshazzar

53. He prophesied bondage for Paul (Acts 21:10)
55. Bear or bee
56. Included in the inheritance of the tribe of Asher (Joshua 19:27)

DOWN

1. He was "smote" by Jael (Judges 4)
2. Clara Bow, the ____ Girl
3. City near Bethel
4. Part of the hemoglobin molecule
5. Wife of Joseph (Genesis 41)
6. "Say ____"
7. ____ it on
8. Single
9. ____ a roll
10. Prettier
11. City in Assyria (Genesis 10:11)
13. Cattle crowds
16. Arabian city (Isaiah 21)
20. Brother of Joab (1 Chronicles 2:16)
21. Assign worth to (arch.)
22. Palm or line
23. "He that hath a bountiful ____ shall be blessed" (Proverbs 22:9)
26. Son of Zerahiah (Ezra 8:4)
29. Relative of a borough (abbr.)
31. Son of Jether (1 Chronicles 7:38)
33. Alleviated

34. Servant of Gideon (Judges 7:10)
36. Middle Eastern language (abbr.)
37. City in the inheritance of the children of Simeon (Joshua 19:4)
39. Southern European country
40. His son Jonathan served in David's army (1 Chronicles 11:34)
41. Asiatic deer (pl.)
44. Linking verb
45. Comparative conjunction
48. Get-together, for a purpose
51. Favorite first word?
52. Preposition

54. Command word

PUZZLE 6

Teri Grottke

ACROSS

1. Cake mix maker (last name)
6. Amasses
11. Store under pressure
12. Has (arch.)
14. Conjunction
15. Touched
17. City near Bethel
18. Military abbr.
19. Marian, et al.
20. Chemical element (abbr.)
21. N.T. book (abbr.)
23. Gilded or Jazz
24. Son of Jether (1 Chronicles 7:38)
25. Wipe away (arch.)
28. Ammonite who invaded Jabeshgilead (1 Samuel 11:1)
31. More than one orthopedist (abbr.)
32. Normal, but maybe not for Nicklaus
33. "For the ____ shall be prosperous" (Zechariah 8:12)
35. "Smote all their enemies with the ____ of the sword" (Esther 9:5)
38. Familiar cavern sight
40. Exclamation
42. Son of Elishama (1 Chronicles 7:27)
43. I ____ (Jehovah)
44. Struck (arch.)
46. Laughing sound
47. Eastern seaboard state (abbr.)
48. Worn by the disciples, among others
50. Simile word
51. Hackneyed
53. Son of Reuel (Genesis 36:13)
55. ____ days
56. "A Sceptre shall. . .destroy all the children of ____" (Numbers 24:17)

DOWN

1. Dread
2. Pronoun
3. ____ degree
4. Son of Shem (Genesis 10:22)
5. Family of returning exiles (Ezra 2:35)
6. Grasp (arch.)
7. Some of Bo-Peep's brood?
8. Conjunction
9. Required subject in school (abbr.)
10. Escalator option
11. Room or walk
13. Judah stayed with him in Adullam (Genesis 38:1)
16. Archaeological site
22. In the course of
24. Brother of Moses
26. Before (poet.)
27. Double this for a deadly fly
29. Likely
30. Laughing sound
34. Condemned

35. Belonging to the evil one
36. Son of Levi (Genesis 46:11)
37. Son of Seth
    (1 Chronicles 1:1)
38. Prohibit
39. Wrong
41. Son of Zophah
    (1 Chronicles 7:37)
44. Father of Heber (Luke 3:35)
45. King of Israel, son of
    Baasha (1 Kings 16:8)
48. "Gal" of songdom
49. Pronoun
52. 'Bye, to Brits
54. Preposition

PUZZLE 7

Teri Grottke

ACROSS

1. Regal
6. "Beeroth of the children of ____" (Deuteronomy 10:6)
11. Pronoun
12. "A workman that ____ not to be ashamed" (2 Timothy 2:15)
14. Dir.
15. Hot ____
17. O.T. book
19. Medical abbr. for delirious state
20. Tyre and ____
21. Son of Aram (Genesis 10:23)
23. Yes!
24. Arsenic (abbr.)
26. "As thou goest unto ____ a mount of the east" (Genesis 10:30)
30. Another name for Hagar
34. Son of Midian (Genesis 25:4)
35. ____ wave
36. Jesse's third son (1 Chronicles 2:13)
38. Name that means "son of my sorrow"
39. Note on diatonic scale
40. "Where his tent had been. . . between Beth-el and ____" (Genesis 13:3)
42. Linking verb
43. O.T. book (abbr.)
46. Wheat by-product

50. Ignore
51. Expiates
53. ____ art
54. In nearest proximity
56. Pronoun
58. What to do with rosebuds?
59. Reposed

DOWN

1. Chess piece (abbr.)
2. Possessive pronoun
3. Insect
4. Some tennis serves
5. Biblical pronoun
6. Warrior in David's army (1 Chronicles 12:6)
7. Site of threshing floor where Joseph mourned Jacob (Genesis 50:10)
8. Son of Abinadab (2 Samuel 6:3)
9. Furniture tree
10. Dir.
13. Basketball pass (colloq.)
16. Masculine nickname
18. Article
21. Biblical verb
22. Son of Eliphaz (1 Chronicles 1:36)
23. Capital of Moab (Numbers 21:15)
24. Naaman preferred this river in Damascus to the Jordan (2 Kings 5:12)
25. Near where John the Baptist baptized (John 3:23)
27. Greek letter

28. Part of a garment
29. Band or chair
31. Consumed
32. Cotton ____
33. Fuss
37. Sighing sound
38. Grievous
41. King of Judah, et al. (I Kings 15:8)
43. Preposition
44. So extreme
45. Competent
47. Tea, for one
48. Picnic pests
49. The royal ____
50. Retreat, for some
52. Pronoun used for a country

53. King of Bashan (Numbers 21:33)
55. Conjunction
57. "Mr. ____" of TV fame

PUZZLE 8

Teri Grottke

ACROSS

1. Dignity
6. Solomon's throne had six of these (2 Chronicles 9:18)
11. What Benjamin was first named (Genesis 35:18)
12. Trusts (arch.)
14. Son of Aram (Genesis 10:23)
15. Brother of Rephah (1 Chronicles 7:25)
17. City near Bethel (Joshua 7:2)
18. O.T. book. (one of two, abbr.)
19. Stickers
20. Union Pacific, e.g.
21. Airport code on the Big Island
23. "Of Keros, the children of____" (Nehemiah 7:47)
24. Son of Jether (1 Chronicles 7:38)
25. Baby
28. One of Levites named in the book of the kings (1 Chronicles 9:15)
31. Mountain (comb. form)
32. "They have gone in the way of Cain, and ____ greedily" (Jude 11)
33. Became stable
36. Jesus healed his mother-in-law (Mark 1:30)
39. Biblical verb KJV
40. Fish eggs
42. O.T. bk.
43. Laughing sound
44. Where Abraham pursued those who had captured Lot (Genesis 14:15)
46. ____ a tee
47. Preposition
48. He accompanied Paul into Asia (Acts 20:4)
50. Pronoun
51. Interior or inner part
53. Among the new generation of Israel (pl., Numbers 26:16)
55. Prepared
56. Amorite king (Joshua 10:3)

DOWN

1. Father of Tabrimon (1 Kings 15:18)
2. Subatomic particle (suffix)
3. Conjunction
4. Column name in multidigit addition
5. Got up (arch.)
6. Son of Judah (Genesis 38:5)
7. A1
8. N.T. book (abbr.)
9. Subject taught by a coach? (abbr.)
10. Comics heroine Brenda, and others
11. Son of Jogli (Numbers 34:22)
13. Adullamite who was Judah's friend (Genesis 38:1)
16. City near Bethel (var.) (Joshua 7:2)

22. "Many knew him, and ran ____ thither" (Mark 6:33)
24. John the Baptist baptized here (John 3:23)
26. Masculine nickname
27. "But as the days of ____ were" (Matthew 24:37)
29. "Of ____, the family of the Erites" (Numbers 26:16)
30. Strike with force
33. She hid the Hebrew spies (Joshua 2:1)
34. Keynote speaker
35. Jesus healed a man with this disease on the Sabbath (Luke 14:2)

36. "There, in a portion of the lawgiver, was he ____" (Deuteronomy 33:21)
37. Lying below the earth's surface
38. The ____ of the Fisherman (West novel)
41. O.T. minor prophet (abbr., var.)
44. Out or over
45. There's companion
48. Baltic, for example
49. Tease
52. "As ____ forgive our debtors" (Matthew 6:12)
54. Note on the diatonic scale

PUZZLE 9

Teri Grottke

ACROSS

1. The great I ____
3. Stay and chat
8. Article
10. Son of Dishan (Genesis 36:28)
12. Son of Shemaiah (1 Chronicles 26:7)
13. Santa's sound
14. "Today shalt thou be with me in ____" (Luke 23:43)
16. "____ paint"
17. "I see"
18. Minor prophet (abbr.)
19. Electrical abbr.
21. Linking verb
22. "____ hath good report of all men" (3 John 12)
25. Single bill
27. Hence
28. Hospital inits.
29. Continent (abbr.)
31. Brother of Shoham (1 Chronicles 24:27)
33. Middle Eastern crop
35. Capital of Moab (Numbers 21:15)
36. Exists
38. Chemical symbol for tin (abbr.)
39. Acorn tree
40. Ooze
42. Handles clumsily
44. Grain (Isaiah 28:25)
46. City near Bethel (Joshua 7:2)
47. Commercial spelling of a word that means facile
48. Preposition
50. Retirement acct.
51. Returning Jew from exile (Nehemiah 7:7)
55. The Holy Spirit wouldn't let Paul and Silas go here (Acts 16:7)
58. Manna measure
59. Understanding
60. Masculine nickname

DOWN

1. Son of Ulla (1 Chronicles 7:39)
2. Disfigure
3. Expresses
4. Possessive pronoun
5. Cut off
6. Preposition
7. Electronics giant (abbr.)
8. "Ir, and Hushim, the sons of ____" (1 Chronicles 7:12)
9. Memo
10. Away from (prefix)
11. "That at the ____ of Jesus" (Philippians 2:10)
15. Unclear
16. Used to be
20. Sky, to Simone
22. Family room
23. Dressed ____ the nines
24. Eastern U.S. university (abbr.)
25. Minor prophet (var., abbr.)
26. Abner's father (1 Samuel 14:51)

29. What a veteran is
30. Question
32. Slick or skin
33. Atop
34. Promise
37. "Of Keros, the children of
____" (Nehemiah 7:47)
38. Dir.
40. Box ____
41. Nation God called against
Babylon
(Jeremiah 51:27)
42. "The Princess and the
____" (classic fairy tale)
43. "The border shall fetch a
compass from ____"
(Numbers 34:5)

44. It may stick out on Olive
Oyl
45. Son of Bela
(1 Chronicles 7:7)
49. Christmas tree
52. A city of Judah
(Joshua 15:32)
53. Minor prophet (abbr.)
54. Church denomination
(abbr.)
56. Masculine pronoun
57. "____ cannot serve God
and mammon"
(Matthew 6:24)

PUZZLE 10

Teri Grottke

ACROSS

1. Shoe parts
6. Greek form of Uzziah
11. Son of Levi (Genesis 46:11)
12. Father of Baruch (Jeremiah 32:12)
14. Masculine nickname
15. Son of Adiel (1 Chronicles 9:12)
17. School subj.
18. Vote
19. Father of Darda (1 Kings 4:31)
20. Pronoun
21. Family of returned exiles (Ezra 2:57)
23. Pilot makes one
24. ____ change
25. Assign (arch.)
28. They come in flights
31. Slangy denial
32. It gives a hoot
33. Cauterized
36. Address
39. ____ blond
40. Construction necessity (abbr.)
42. Jane ____
43. Phonetic sound
44. Exhibits
46. Hospital inits.
47. "The kingdom of heaven is ____ hand" (Matthew 3:2)
48. Son of Elioenai (1 Chronicles 3:24)
50. Biblical exclamation
51. Catch one's eye
53. Glided
55. What Simeon was called at Antioch (Acts 13:1)
56. "The heifer. . .which is neither ____ nor sown" (Deuteronomy 21:4)

DOWN

1. Greek form of Sodom
2. Buckeye state (abbr.)
3. O.T. book (abbr.)
4. "He [Samson]. . .dwelt in the top of the rock ____" (Judges 15:8)
5. Son of Jahdai (1 Chronicles 2:47)
6. What the Israelites missed in the wilderness (Numbers 11:15)
7. Ardor
8. Son of Bela (1 Chronicles 7:7)
9. City near Bethel (Joshua 7:2)
10. "Pass ye away, thou inhabitant of ____" (Micah 1:11)
11. Early descendant of Adam (1 Chronicles 1:2)
13. What a good dog does
16. Pronoun for a seafaring vessel
22. Son of Asher (1 Chronicles 7:30)
24. Bribed
26. Wax or wig
27. Article
29. Big ____

30. Reverence
33. Antichrist
34. Son of Mehir
    (1 Chronicles 4:11)
35. Merchant
36. Contention
37. Became aloof
38. "When ____. . .had heard
    these things, he was trou-
    bled" (Matthew 2:3)
41. "Of Keros, the children of
    ____" (Nehemiah 7:47)
44. Visage
45. Father of Heber (Luke 3:35)
48. Verb for flower child
49. Mount where Aaron died
    (Numbers 20:25-29)

52. Polynesian woody plant
54. I (pl.)

PUZZLE 11

Teri Grottke

ACROSS

1. Stop! (arch.)
3. Son of Tahath (1 Chronicles 6:24)
8. Father of Simon Peter (John 1:42)
10. Assyrian god, which had a house in Nineveh (2 Kings 19:37)
13. Jealous gems?
15. Nephew of Abraham
17. Pronoun
18. Linking verb
19. Home of the brave (abbr.)
21. Postermer state
22. Reproved
25. "In the night ____ of Moab is laid waste" (Isaiah 15:1)
27. Dir.
28. Where Miami University is (abbr.)
29. Hectare (abbr.)
31. Of starch (comb. form)
33. Pilfers (colloq.)
35. Musical abbr.
36. Where "The Music Man" was set (abbr.)
38. Figure on many TV crime shows (abbr.)
39. Hardwood
40. Son of Joktan (Genesis 10:26)
42. Son of Salah (Genesis 10:24)
44. Exclamation
46. Metric abbr.
47. Part of middle-school curriculum (abbr.)
48. Word in a command
50. Big ____, CA
51. Age of Jehoiachin when he began his reign
55. Deception
58. Too
59. Commanded
60. Strike

DOWN

1. Domicile
2. Chemical suffix
3. Except that
4. To free, with "of "
5. Assign
6. Hesitation sound
7. Biblical exclamation
8. "He is a ____, which is one inwardly" (Romans 2:29)
9. Son of Ulla (1 Chronicles 7:39)
11. Attired
12. O.T. minor prophet (abbr.)
14. First name of famed football coach
16. Symbol of thorium
20. "As ____ in summer. . .so honour is not seemly" (Proverbs 26:1)
22. ____, the Beloved Country (Paton book)
23. Preposition

24. Son of Benjamin
    (Genesis 46:21)
25. Eleventh letter of the
    Hebrew alphabet
26. Mischievous child
29. Was told, KJV style
30. Question
32. Untruth
33. Where Durban is (abbr.)
34. Nineteenth-century
    American writer
37. Prepare for battle
38. AL lineup abbr.
40. Assyrian king mentioned in
    Hosea (Hosea 5:13)
41. Alter
42. N.T. epistle (abbr.)

43. City where David took
    "exceeding much brass"
    (2 Samuel 8:8)
44. Snake
45. With Aaron, he held up
    Moses' arms
    (Exodus 17:2)
49. City built by descendants
    of Benjamin
    (1 Chronicles 8:12)
52. To cause to be
    (suffix, Brit.)
53. Book of the Torah (abbr.)
54. Father of Hophni
56. Note of the diatonic scale
57. Singer Ames

PUZZLE 12

Janet W. Adkins

ACROSS

1. Priestly garments
5. "Except your righteousness shall ____ the righteousness of the scribes" (Matthew 5:20)
7. Linking verb
8. Replied
10. "Give unto the Lord the glory ____ unto his name" (Psalm 29:2)
11. "Can a maid forget her ornaments, or a bride her ____?" (Jeremiah 2:32)
13. Of flying (comb. form)
14. Son of Seth
15. "Israel did ____ manna forty years" (Exodus 16:35)
17. "Yea, the ____ hath found an house" (Psalm 84:3)
19. "Employer" of Hagar
21. Oft-used abbr.
22. One (Ger.)
23. Rate of speed (abbr.)
24. Where Montauk is (abbr.)
25. "All they that cast ____ into the brooks shall lament" (Isaiah 19:8)
27. "They ____ in thee, and were not confounded" (Psalm 22:5)
29. "Agnus ___"
30. Pay attention
31. "Yet will I bring ____ plague more upon Pharaoh" (Exodus 11:1)
32. "____ ye, and believe the gospel" (Mark 1:15)
34. "And Nathan said to David, Thou ____ the man" (2 Samuel 12:7)
35. End or line
36. John, to a Scot
37. "He made a ____ about the altar" (1 Kings 18:32)
39. "He shall be like a ____ planted by the rivers" (Psalm 1:3)

DOWN

1. Chopping tool
2. Public national library (abbr.)
3. "Upon these we ____ more abundant honour" (1 Corinthians 12:23)
4. "He hath put down the mighty from their ____" (Luke 1:52)
5. Before (poet.)
6. 502, according to Cicero
7. Charismatic atmosphere
9. God spoke in Bible times through these
10. Rely
11. Immediately (arch.)
12. Serving of corn
13. "All they which dwelt in ____ heard the word of the Lord Jesus" (Acts 19:10)
14. Great Lake
16. "I was afraid, and went and hid thy ____ in the earth" (Matthew 25:25)

18. Trusted, with "upon"
19. Potato
20. "I flee unto thee to _____ me" (Psalm 143:9)
23. "_____ not thyself because of evildoers" (Psalm 37:1)
26. European lang.
27. "Leah was _____ eyed" (Genesis 29:17)
28. Ripped
30. "If thou seek him with all thy _____" (Deuteronomy 4:29)
33. Favorite
34. Sighing sound

36. "He casteth forth his _____ like morsels" (Psalm 147:17)
38. Compass dir.

PUZZLE 13

Janet W. Adkins

ACROSS

1. Belonging to the Jairite who "was a chief ruler about David" (2 Samuel 20:26)
5. Lures
7. "Even of your lusts that ____ in your members" (James 4:1)
8. Name for a boy in Barcelona?
10. French export, to Emile
11. Really (arch.)
13. "Without the word be ____ by the conversation of the wives" (1 Peter 3:1)
14. New cars on the road
15. Person concerned with (suffix)
17. "But the righteous into life ____" (Matthew 25:46)
19. Advantage
21. City near Bethel
22. Electric ____
23. "But ____ thing is needful" (Luke 10:42)
24. Irish Pop
25. "And put a ____ to thy throat" (Proverbs 23:2)
27. "If he that cometh preacheth ____ Jesus" (2 Corinthians 11:4)
29. Ford model
30. Formerly Persia
31. Shem's home, for a while
32. Prayer
34. Hirt, and others
35. Region in NE Poland with many lakes (abbr.)
36. Like alt.
37. Person afflicted with tuberculosis (colloq.)
39. "Esau, who is ____ " (Genesis 36:1)

DOWN

1. Noun-forming suffix
2. Paper measure (abbr.)
3. "I ____ unto Caesar" (Acts 25:11)
4. "I will exalt my throne above the ____ of God" (Isaiah 14:13)
5. To M.D.s, summer scourge
6. Middle-school subj.
7. "Do not drink ____ nor strong drink" (Leviticus 10:9)
9. Bible mount
10. November activity
11. "Then Samuel took a ____ of oil" (1 Samuel 10:1)
12. Biblical exclamation
13. "All knees shall be ____ as water" (Ezekiel 21:7)
14. Joint
16. ____ of the Purple Sage (Z. Grey book)
18. Change for the better
19. In the very near future (arch.)
20. Whim
23. Second son of Judah (Genesis 38:4)
26. Certain California judge

27. In the vicinity
28. "How long _____ ye between two opinions" (1 Kings 18:21)
30. Release
33. Suitable for (suffix)
34. Farm science (comb. form)
36. "They might only touch the _____ of his garment" (Matthew 14:36)
38. Word in the Great Commission

PUZZLE 14

Michael J. Landi

ACROSS

1. Place which means "well of the oath" (Genesis 21: 30-33))
6. Compass dir.
8. Prophet who advised David to go into the land of Judah (1 Samuel 22:5)
9. U.S. site of a Summer Olympics (abbr.)
10. Where Paul healed Publius' father (var., Acts 28:1-8)
11. Judah thought this woman was a prostitute (Genesis 38)
12. Electrical abbr.
13. City also known as Lydda (1 Chronicles 8:12)
16. Where one finds "the street which is called Straight"
17. "He is of ____; ask him" (John 9:21)
18. Esther's Shusan (var.)
20. Pot adjunct
21. City near Bethel (var.)
22. Coral reef
23. Consumed
25. The Great I ____
28. Site of Jesus' first miracle on earth
30. "The Nethinims dwelt in ____, unto the place over against the water gate" (Nehemiah 3:26)
31. "____ sharpeneth ____" [word repeated] (Proverbs 27:17)
34. Right-hand page (abbr.)
35. "For this Agar is mount Sinai in ____" (Galatians 4:25)
37. "David. . .escaped to the cave ____" (1 Samuel 22:1)
39. His two sons, Hophni and Phinehas, were priests of the Lord
41. Cape Cod state (abbr.)
42. After this Bible book, God did not speak to His people for 400 years (abbr.)
43. River of Egypt
45. "In so doing thou shalt ____ coals of fire on his head" (Romans 12:20)
46. Shammah was the son of this Hararite (2 Samuel 23:11)
47. Lion of ____ (name of Jesus)
48. "Arise ye, and let us go up to ____ unto the Lord our God" (var., Jeremiah 31:6)
51. Extremely agitated
52. Understand
53. Like a mom's day
54. "The Lord will cut off from ____ head and tail, branch and rush" (Isaiah 9:14)

DOWN

1. Where the handicapped waited "for the moving of the water" (John 5:2)
2. Destination of two disciples, when they were joined by the risen Jesus Christ (Luke 24:13)
3. One of seven cities addressed in early chapters of Revelation
4. "I was at Shushan. . .in the province of ____" (Daniel 8:2)
5. "Who passing through the valley of ____ make it a well" (Psalm 84:6)
6. Continent (abbr.)
7. Son of Shaphan (Jeremiah 29:3)

8. Paul stopped here on his third missionary journey, after Antioch (Acts 18:23)
10. Home of Gaius and Aristarchus, two of Paul's companions (Acts 19:29)
14. King who was a remnant of giants (Deuteronomy 3:11)
15. A city of Lycaonia, where Paul fled after Iconium (Acts 14:6)
19. "The field of blood" (Acts 1:19)
20. Where the city of Myra was located (Acts 27:5)
24. Famous seaport on the Mediterranean, in Bible days (var., Ezekiel 26)
26. Shape
27. City where Lydia was converted (Acts 16:12-15)

29. "All thy fortresses shall be spoiled, as Shalman spoiled Beth-____" (Hosea 10:14)
32. In a parable, five virgins forgot this (Matthew 25:3)
33. Widow of ____ (Luke 7:11-18)
36. Where Paul spent his last days
37. Site of Mars' hill (Acts 17:22)
38. Wise men
40. Where Abraham built his second altar (Genesis 12:8)
44. ____ ink
47. N.T. book (abbr.)
48. Dir.
49. Branch of medicine (abbr.)
50. Greek letter
51. "Hearken unto the voice of ____ cry" (Psalm 5:2)

PUZZLE 15

Teri Grottke

ACROSS

1. "For they considered not the ____ of the loaves" (Mark 6:52)
7. "In the days of Noah, while the ____ was a-preparing" (1 Peter 3:20)
10. "The sons of Carmi; ____" (1 Chronicles 2:7)
11. Word in a command
12. U.S. state named after Elizabeth I (abbr.)
13. Where the action is
14. "Those that walk in pride he is able to ____" (Daniel 4:37)
16. What the wife of Phinehas named their son (1 Samuel 4:21)
18. Father of Eliud (Matthew 1:14)
20. City near Bethel
22. "Thy right ____ shall save me" (Psalm 138:7)
23. Used to make powder
24. "Let tears run down like a river. . .give thyself no ____" (Lamentations 2:18)
26. Former name of Bethel (Genesis 28:19)
28. "The rock poured me out ____ of oil" (Job 29:6)
32. "As he saith also in ____" (Romans 9:25)
34. Waif, often
35. Compass dir.
36. Related to the camel
38. Forty-niner's destination (abbr.)
39. Father of Ahihud (Numbers 34:27)
41. ____ what?
42. State on the Pacific (abbr.)
43. Redact
44. Roger Williams's state (abbr.)
46. Reach out and touch someone (abbr.)
47. "I ____ hath sent me unto you" (Exodus 3:14)
48. Frustrate
50. "And on the wall of ____ he [Jotham] built much" (2 Chronicles 27:3)
52. "Yet had he the ____ of the spirit" (Malachi 2:15)

DOWN

1. "Is therefore Christ the ____ of sin? God forbid" (Galatians 2:17)
2. Chemical symbol
3. "I am glad of the coming of . . .Fortunatus and ____" (1 Corinthians 16:17)
4. Small fish used as bait
5. Political party in Great Britain
6. Where life and death decisions are made (abbr.)
7. As sons of God, what we can call Him (Galatians 4:6)
8. Stretch
9. Parent

12. "Surely there is a _____ for the silver" (Job 28:1)
15. Where the Emims were smote, in _____ Kiriathaim (Genesis 14:5)
17. "_____ be thy name" (Luke 11:2)
19. Atlantic seaboard state (abbr.)
21. "And Phares begat _____" (Matthew 1:3)
25. Son of Japheth (1 Chronicles 1:5)
27. Simon _____ (Acts 1:13)
29. Exec.
30. "The Lord make the woman that is come into thine house like _____" (Ruth 4:11)

31. Slow goer
33. Shade tree
35. Son of Noah
37. "To meet the Lord in the _____" (1 Thessalonians 4:17)
40. "He that eateth of this bread shall _____ for ever" (John 6:58)
45. Borrower's woe
46. "In all matters of wisdom. . . the king. . .found them _____ times better" (Daniel 1:20)
47. Simile syntax
49. Greek letter
51. Part of middle-school curriculum (abbr.)

PUZZLE 16

Beverly Barnes

ACROSS

1. "We have seen his _____ in the east" (Matthew 2:2)
5. Accepts, in a way
9. Atlantic seaboard state (abbr.)
11. "My _____ is in thee" (Psalm 39:7)
12. Warehouse
13. "Keep me as the _____ of the eye" (Psalm 17:8)
15. _____ de France
17. "My _____ shall praise thee" (Psalm 63:3)
19. Addiction to (suffix)
22. Affirmative (colloq.)
23. "Make thee a fiery serpent, and set it upon a _____" (Numbers 21:8)
24. Printer's measure
26. Secondborn of Adam
30. Cambridge college (abbr.)
31. "At thy word I will let down the _____" (Luke 5:5)
33. One source of evil
35. "The Lord is thy _____ upon thy right hand" (Psalm 121:5)
38. Soloist
39. Peter or Paul (abbr.)
41. Book or teller
42. "The sceptre shall not depart from _____ " (Genesis 49:10)
44. "As light of foot as a wild _____" (2 Samuel 2:18)
45. Oft-used abbr.
46. "Put ye in the sickle, for the harvest is _____" (Joel 3:13)
48. Stay _____
50. "Thou hast been a _____ for me, and a strong tower" (Psalm 61:3)
52. _____ is condition
53. Unit of dry measure (abbr.)
54. Complete set of events
55. "Our word. . .was not yea and _____" (2 Corinthians 1:18)
56. Sauce made with fresh basil
57. Duly noted at a yearly physical (abbr.)

DOWN

1. Hone
2. Hat or heavy
3. "_____ thine heart to understanding" (Proverbs 2:2)
4. Depended upon
5. Second letter of the Hebrew alphabet (var.)
6. "They that wait _____ the Lord shall renew their strength" (Isaiah 40:31)
7. Thou, to a non-Quaker
8. Dismantle
10. Masculine nickname
14. Gov't. agency
16. "Consider the _____ of the field" (Matthew 6:28)
18. "Endured the cross, despising the _____" (Hebrews 12:2)
20. _____ cat

21. "A city that is ____ on an hill" (Matthew 5:14)
25. "As an eagle stirreth up her ____" (Deuteronomy 32:11)
27. One who takes to the rails (colloq.)
28. "Bread ____ and to spare" (Luke 15:17)
29. What a bank may do
32. Paul's ____ in the flesh
34. "For there is a ____ sacrifice there for all the family" (1 Samuel 20:6)
36. City on the banks of the Arnon River (Joshua 13:16)
37. Changed hues

40. "Over ____" (wartime favorite)
41. "Get thee behind me, ____" (Luke 4:8)
42. Prince of Peace
43. Wed, in Dogpatch
47. Throw things at
49. "Land of the free" (abbr.)
51. System or sphere
53. "____ of good cheer; I have overcome the world" (John 16:33)

PUZZLE 17

Michael J. Landi

ACROSS

1. "There is nothing from without a man, that entering. . .can ____ him" (Mark 7:15)
4. "At home in the body, we are ____ from the Lord" (2 Corinthians 5:6)
8. Article
9. "____ your enemies" (Matthew 5:44)
11. "Thy rod and thy ____ they comfort me" (Psalm 23:4)
14. "The captain of his host was Abner, the son of ____" (1 Samuel 14:50)
15. "The Lord hath made bare his holy ____" (Isaiah 52:10)
16. "As a ____ doth gather her brood" (Luke 13:34)
17. Celebrated city of Asia Minor, visited by Paul more than once (Acts 13:51)
18. ____ of Sharon (Song of Solomon 2:1)
20. "The ____ is not to the swift" (Ecclesiastes 9:11)
22. "At the name of Jesus every ____ should bow" (Philippians 2:10)
24. Denial (arch.)
26. Part of a castle
27. "Who can utter the mighty ____ of the Lord?" (Psalm 106:2)
28. King of Israel who was killed by Zimri (var., 1 Kings 16:6-10)
29. Linking verb
32. "If any of you lack wisdom, let him ____ of God" (James 1:5)
33. "If thou wilt ____ into life, keep the commandments" (Matthew 19:17)
34. From 1 Corinthians 13: faith, hope, and ____
36. Idol worshiped by Jezebel, among many others (1 Kings 16:31)
37. Hard ____
40. Not B.C.
41. "Which he ____ on us abundantly through Jesus Christ" (Titus 3:6)
43. Judah's firstborn (Genesis 38:7)
44. Therefore

DOWN

1. "Lest at any time thou ____ thy foot against a stone" (Matthew 4:6)
2. "When thou prayest, ____ into thy closet" (Matthew 6:6)
3. ____ Al, airline known for its security measures
4. "____ not yourselves, but rather give place unto wrath" (Romans 12:19)
5. Son of Zophah (1 Chronicles 7:36)

6. "But let a man _____ him self" 1 Corinthians 11:28)

7. "The tongue can no man _____" (James 3:8)

10. City of Benjamin built or restored by Shamed (1 Chronicles 8:12)

12. "Arise, ye princes, and _____ the shield" (Isaiah 21:5)

13. How to describe Nebuchadnezzar's furnace

19. "The _____ for height, and the earth for depth" (Proverbs 25:3)

21. "Tarsus, a city in _____" (Acts 21:39)

22. Map info

23. "As also in all his _____, speaking in them of these things" (2 Peter 3:16)

25. Past somnolent

30. "For the _____ is red and lowering" (Matthew 16:3)

31. Gypsy _____ (sight in big city)

32. Father of Saul's concubine (2 Samuel 3:7)

35. "Be not _____ with thy mouth" (Ecclesiastes 5:2)

38. Neh. is part of this

39. Biblical pronoun

42. "Of all that Jesus began both to _____ and teach" (Acts 1:1)

PUZZLE 18

Michael J. Landi

ACROSS

2. Metamorphosed
10. "He took ____ of his ribs" (Genesis 2:21)
11. Crasher or keeper
12. Partake
13. Missing ingredient in manna
14. Form of "drachma"
16. ____ Aviv
18. "But glory, honour, and __,to every man that worketh good" (Romans 2:10)
20. Pal, to Philippe
21. ____ in (first point scored after deuce?)
22. Loan
24. "Burning ____ and a wicked heart" (Proverbs 26:23)
26. "He revealeth the ____ and secret things" (Daniel 2:22)
28. Conjunction
30. What April brings
32. "The ____ of all Israel are upon thee" (1 Kings 1:20)
34. One of David's men (1 Kings 1:8)
36. "Sow. . .in righteousness, ____ in mercy" (Hosea 10:12)
37. "Enter into the rock. . .for the glory of his ____" (Isaiah 2:10)
39. "But ____ wrought evil in the eyes of the Lord" (1 Kings 16:25)
40. What Isaac named the well at Gerar (Genesis 26:20)
42. Roman emperor with whom Paul had an audience
43. Not A.D.
44. Zaftig, but more bluntly perhaps?
45. "Call me not ____ call me Mara" (Ruth 1:20)
48. "Ye have made the heart of the righteous ____" (Ezekiel 13:22)
49. Aeries

DOWN

1. "Let not sin therefore reign in your ____ body" (Romans 6:12)
2. Do ____!
3. Meal shared by early Christians
4. Hub of a wheel
5. "We pray you in Christ's ____ be ye reconciled" (2 Corinthians 5:20)
6. "____ cities, with walls, gates, and bars" (2 Chronicles 8:5)
7. ____ Sea
8. Feminine name that means "bitter"
9. Rock where Samson lived after slaughter of Philistines (Judges 15:11)
15. "Come, buy wine and ____ without money" (Isaiah 55:1)
17. Enlighten

19. Head of a family of Gad (var., 1 Chronicles 5:13)
23. Runs swiftly
25. "For the _____ things are passed away" (Revelation 21:4)
27. "Learn first to show _____ at home" (1 Timothy 5:4)
29. "To every man that asketh you a _____ of the hope" (1 Peter 3:15)
31. "_____, in all these things we are more than conquerors" (Romans 8:37)
32. Town of the tribe of Dan (Joshua 19:43)
33. Apostles and others

35. At ___-abarim, in the wilderness before Moab, Israelites pitched tents (Numbers 21:11)
38. Chief Philistine city (1 Samuel 6:17)
41. New Testament book
46. Its capital is Augusta (abbr.)
47. "For God _____ my witness" (Romans 1:9)

PUZZLE 19

Michael J. Landi

ACROSS

1. Saul fought against them (1 Samuel 14:47)
6. "There shall they rehearse the righteous ____ of the Lord" (Judges 5:11)
9. "He shall ____ with his teeth, and melt away" (Psalm 112:10)
10. Actress McDaniel
11. "My ____ shall be joyful in my God" (Isaiah 61:10)
12. "Out of thine hand the ____ of trembling" (Isaiah 51:22)
14. Word heard on movie sets
15. Preposition
16. "By the rivers of Babylon, there we ____" (Psalm 137:1)
17. Land of Job
20. "____ unto you, scribes and Pharisees, hypocrites!" (Matthew 23:15)
22. Tenth part of one's income
23. ____ of the Chaldees
24. Town of the tribe of Benjamin (1 Chronicles 8:12)
26. "Go and ____ in the ears of Jerusalem" (Jeremiah 2:2)
27. Joshua, the son of ___ (Exodus 33:11)
28. Gershwin
31. "The Lord make his ____ shine upon thee" (Numbers 6:25)
32. Word with grade or braid
33. Father of Ehud (Judges 3:15)
34. Scale unit (abbr.)
37. ____ Behind (LaHaye/Jenkins book)
38. "All we like ____ have gone astray" (Isaiah 53:6)

DOWN

1. Item worn by the high priest (Exodus 28:4)
2. "Because the Lord loved you, . . .he would keep the ____" (Deuteronomy 7:8)
3. "The tongue is a fire, a world of ____" (James 3:6)
4. Common abbr.
5. "As a jewel of gold in a swine's ____" (Proverbs 11:22)
6. Balaam's beast
7. "They hated knowledge, and did not ____ the fear of the Lord" (Proverbs 1:29)
8. "He went out, and departed into a ____ place" (Mark 1:35)
13. "To see thy ____ and thy glory" (Psalm 63:2)
18. "David took the strong hold of ___: the same is the city of David" (2 Samuel 5:7)
19. Without end
21. Languages (arch.)
23. Father of Michaiah

(2 Chronicles 13:2)
25. Greek letter
29. "If ye have _____ as a grain
    of mustard seed"
    (Matthew 17:20)
30. "I _____ where I sowed not"
    (Matthew 25:26)
35. Nephew of Abraham, the
    son of Nahor
    (Genesis 22:21)
36. Biblical pronoun

PUZZLE 20

Janet Kennedy

ACROSS

1. "There sat a certain man at Lystra, ____ in his feet" (Acts 14:8)
7. Recurring chills
10. "When her branch is yet tender, . . .ye know that summer is ____" (Mark 13:28)
11. At the age of (abbr.)
13. Naaman's illness (2 Kings 5:6)
14. Mischievous child
16. Study of art or science (pl. suffix)
18. Football position (abbr.)
19. Detail for a duffer
20. Stir up
21. Angry
22. Chicago's Lake Shore, for one (abbr.)
23. First name in life preservers?
24. ____ upsmanship
25. ____ Bravo
26. Possessive pronoun
27. "____, and Ammon, and Amalek; the Philistines" (Psalm 83:7)
30. Accountant's abbr.
32. In what state Churchill Downs is found (abbr.)
33. "____ said unto Samuel, Go, lie down" (1 Samuel 3:9)
35. What ____. . . ? (worry wart's favorite question)

36. Small drink
38. "I will not drink henceforth of this fruit of the ____" (Matthew 26:29)
40. Sacrifice site
41. "Yesterday at the seventh hour the ____ left him" (John 4:52)
42. As stated
43. "But the wise took ____ in their vessels" (Matthew 25:4)
44. "Resist the devil, and he will ____ from you" (James 4:7)
45. Female deer (pl.)
46. Organization including Britain, France, and Germany (abbr.)
47. Bring legal action
48. "A certain man. . .had the ____"(Luke 14:2)
49. Egress

DOWN

1. "Himself took our____ and bare our sicknesses" (Matthew 8:17)
2. "Come unto____, all ye that labour" (Matthew 11:28)
3. "And many taken with ____, and that were lame, were healed" (Acts 8:7)
4. Rock worth mining
5. "The man took a golden ____ of half a shekel weight" (Genesis 24:22)

6. Describing a modern take on a classical style
8. Trotting, for one
9. Nero, for one
12. "They. . .fled unto____ and Derbe, cities of Lycaonia" (Acts 14:6)
15. "A merry heart doeth good like a ____" (Proverbs 17:22)
17. ____ of many colors
28. Tournament privilege for number-one ranked team
29. Built to keep a river from overflowing
31. "And Lot dwelled in the ____ of the plain" (Genesis 13:12)
34. "Forsake not the Levite as long as thou ____" (Deuteronomy 12:19)
36. Rigged sailboat
37. Paralysis
39. "Which some professing have ____ concerning the faith" (1 Timothy 6:21)
41. Coming in of the tide
44. Assessment
45. "And whatsoever ye ____ in word or deed" (Colossians 3:17)

PUZZLE 21

Janet Kennedy

ACROSS

1. "Thou breakest the heads of ____ in pieces" (Psalm 74:14)
7. "Every one that lappeth of the water with his tongue, as a ____" (Judges 7:5)
10. In on
11. Like an aria
12. "____ it ever so humble"
13. Conjunction
14. "Behold behind him a ____ caught in a thicket by his horns" (Genesis 22:13)
17. Loathing
18. Feminine nickname
20. Brit. islands (abbr.)
22. Blue pencil pushers? (abbr.)
23. Printer's measure
24. Wisconsin, the ____ State
27. Catch sight of
30. "I ____ the true vine" (John 15:1)
31. "The hart, and the roebuck, and the fallow ____" (Deuteronomy 14:5)
32. "All ____ like sheep have gone astray" (Isaiah 53:6)
34. Rooster's better half
35. Chicago sight
36. Dad, in Dublin
38. One of the 13 original states (abbr.)
39. "Your adversary the devil, as a roaring ____ walketh about" (1 Peter 5:8)
42. Stags
44. What to do with the frizzies and large felines
46. Greek letter
47. Iron (symbol)
48. Verb in primer's vocabulary
50. Director Lupino
52. Kind of engineer (abbr.)
53. TV network
54. "Shalt thou exalt like the horn of an ____" (Psalm 92:10)

DOWN

1. Discovery zone? (abbr.)
2. "The poor man had nothing, save one little ____ lamb" (2 Samuel 12:3)
3. One of the 13 original states (abbr.)
4. "He shall rule. . .with a rod of ____" (Revelation 2:27)
5. Expose to air
6. "And I saw heaven opened, and behold a white ____" (Revelation 19:11)
7. Obstinate one, not too kindly
8. Chemical suffix
9. Rocky Mountain ___
15. Mosquito that carries yellow fever
16. Large quantity
19. Preposition
20. "Easier for a ____ to go through the eye of a needle" (Matthew 19:24)
21. Part of psyche

24. Requested (arch.)
25. "She maketh fine linen, . . . and delivereth _____ unto the merchant" (Proverbs 31:24)
26. Harsh
28. Penn's pad? (abbr.)
29. "The king doth not fetch home again his _____" (2 Samuel 14:13)
33. Exclamation of scorn
34. Tortoise's tormentor
37. City near Bethel
40. These may be yoked
41. Division of the United Kingdom (abbr.)

43. "And Peter followed _____ off" (Luke 22:54)
45. Fuss
49. Good or well (prefix)
50. Characteristic of (suffix)
51. Word in a command

PUZZLE 22

Evelyn M. Boyington

ACROSS

1. Chop off
4. One of Hezekiah's over-seers (2 Chronicles 31:13)
9. One's own turf?
12. Mother of Hezekiah (2 Kings 18:2)
13. Kind of finish
14. "The ____ appeareth, and the tender grass showeth itself" (Proverbs 27:25)
15. Atlantic seaboard state (abbr.)
16. Altar end of a church
17. "When I ____ the five loaves among five thousand" (Mark 8:19)
19. New churches, evangelically speaking
21. "As for ____, he made havoc of the church" (Acts 8:3)
22. "I go my ____ and ye shall seek me" (John 8:21)
23. Paul or Peter or John or...
26. "A river went out of ____ to water the garden" (Genesis 2:10)
28. "Serve him in sincerity and in ____" (Joshua 24:14)
29. Masculine nickname
30. City in central Israel
31. "And Abram passed through the land...unto the plain of ____" (Genesis 12:6)
32. In the ____
33. Jesus conversed in this language when on earth (abbr.)
34. "Eldad and ____ do prophesy in the camp" (Numbers 11:27)
35. "I will give thee a crown of ____" (Revelation 2:10)
36. Day of baptism (two words)
38. Kitchen implement
39. Vainly
40. Progenitor
43. Number of men who met Abraham at his tent, including the Lord (Genesis 18)
45. ____ in full
46. Conjunction
47. Consume
48. Desire strongly
50. Jane or John
51. "He planteth an ____, and the rain doth nourish it" (Isaiah 44:14)
52. Gluts
53. "For ye are all ____ in Christ" (Galatians 3:28)

DOWN

1. "Thy word is a ____ unto my feet" (Psalm 119:105)
2. "And Joktan begat...____ and Abimael and Sheba" (Genesis 10:26,28)
3. Greek letter
4. "The Lord hath brought me home again ____" (Ruth 1:21)
5. Girl in Glasgow
6. Resident (suffix)
7. ____ al
8. "And ___, and Shilhim, ... all the cities are twenty and nine" (Joshua 15:32)
9. Biblical verb
10. "Ye shall be as an ____ whose leaf fadeth" (Isaiah 1:30)
11. What to do with eggs?

16. One among the covenant sealers (Nehemiah 10:26)
18. Make haste
20. Held in fear
21. Flowed or gushed out (O.T. spelling)
23. "Women adorn themselves . . .not with. . .costly ____" (1 Timothy 2:9)
24. Gold ____
25. Life on the ____ (Dobson book)
26. Ardor
27. Feminine name
28. "Exhort one another daily, while it is called ____" (Hebrews 3:13)
31. Samplings of songs?
32. "Whoso breaketh an hedge, a serpent shall ____ him" (Ecclesiastes 10:8)

34. Darius the ____ (Daniel 11:1)
35. Master
37. "The voice of ____, and the voice of gladness" (Jeremiah 7:34)
38. Symptoms of malaise
40. "She shall shave her head, and ____ her nails" (Deuteronomy 21:12)
41. "I will cause the sun to go down at ____" (Amos 8:9)
42. The ____ of life (Revelation 22:2)
43. Prince of Wales, for example
44. Owns
45. Stand ____
49. Apiece (abbr.)
50. Accomplish

PUZZLE 23

Evelyn M. Boyington

ACROSS

1. Cry
4. Dream or organ
8. ____ team
12. Mouth (pl.)
13. "The children of ____ of Hezekiah, ninety and eight" (Ezra 2:16)
14. Jewelry setting, with no metal showing
15. By means of
16. Nurture
17. Great Lake
18. Masculine name that is an amalgam of Abraham and Noah
20. Make ____
22. Prim and proper
24. In Arthurian legend, the wife of Geraint
25. Writing ____ (what Zacharias asked for in Luke 1:63)
26. "____ thou not unto his [God's] words" (Proverbs 30:6)
27. Gazelle
30. Biblical exclamation
31. Possessive pronoun
32. "Thou hast enlarged my steps. . .that my feet did not ____" (Psalm 18:36)
33. Affirmative
34. Compass pt.
35. Obeys, to an AKC member
36. He was a prisoner on Patmos
37. Obliterate
38. Stick
41. Mentally acute
42. Not present and unaccounted for (abbr., pl.)
43. What commandos do
45. Anger
48. Parchment shade
49. "He. . .saw others standing ____ in the marketplace" (Matthew 20:3)
50. Not (prefix)
51. "And they straightway left their ____, and followed him" (Matthew 4:20)
52. Minister to
53. Our Father

DOWN

1. Absorb
2. Crude metal
3. He accompanied Paul on his first missionary journey
4. Procession
5. Article on a list
6. Legume
7. Missions
8. ____ trap
9. Give notice
10. Like many golfers?
11. What to wear when golfing? (pl.)
19. Nard, olive, et al.
21. Word that precedes day or air

22. Between check-in and check-out
23. "We spend our years as a _____ that is told" (Psalm 90:9)
24. All gone!
27. "Yet _____ grapes shall be left in it, as the shaking of an olive tree" (Isaiah 17:6)
28. Sesame, canola, et al.
29. Usually the east end of a church
31. "For such as be blessed of him shall _____ the earth" (Psalm 37:22)
32. Arid
34. Conjunction

35. Noticed
36. "Even so, come, Lord _____" (Revelation 22:20)
38. So be it
39. Prepare vegetables for cooking
40. "As the _____ panteth after the water" (Psalm 42:1)
41. Oven
44. Fruit drink
46. One of Pooh's pals
47. "And then shall the _____ come" (Matthew 24:14)

PUZZLE 24

Evelyn M. Boyington

ACROSS

1. Western state (abbr.)
3. "I gave Egypt for thy ransom, Ethiopia and ____ for thee" (Isaiah 43:3)
7. To do much better than another
12. ____ of the Chaldees
13. From ____ to stern
14. Fabric used to make an ephod
15. In law, an object
17. Preposition
18. "In the beginning was the ____" (John 1:1)
19. "The horse is prepared against the day of ____" (Proverbs 21:31)
21. "Stand in____, and sin not" (Psalm 4:4)
22. "They fled before the men of ____" (Joshua 7:4)
24. Pres. Clinton's home state (abbr.)
25. Simile syntax
26. "The children of Israel be as the ____ of the sea" (Romans 9:27)
28. Administer the SAT again
31. Quaker pronoun
32. You, in the Yucatan
34. Start
36. Provincetown province (abbr.)
37. Grandfather of David, and son of Ruth
40. Means of communication
43. First word written on the wall (Daniel 5)
44. Linking verb
45. "Two of every ____ shalt thou bring into the ark" (Genesis 6:19)
48. Masculine nickname
49. Took a break
51. "It is as high as heaven; . . . ____ than hell" (Job 11:8)
53. Minuscule
54. Naval officer (abbr.)
55. Where one can perspire or be pampered
56. Portion
58. Used by the high priest to hold oil
60. Classified, for one
61. Spread around
62. Altar end of the church
63. Biblical pronoun

DOWN

1. Checks
2. ____ code
3. Christian ed. concern (abbr.)
4. Common abbr.
5. ____ noire
6. "I ____ God, even thy God" (Psalm 50:7)
7. "____ of speech" (how Moses described himself, Exodus 4:10)
8. Employed, in Bible times
9. Conjunction
10. "This I know; for God is for ____" (Psalm 56:9)
11. Printer's measure
16. Day ____
18. "The field is ____, the land mourneth" (Joel 1:10)

20. Three, in Turin
22. "Ramoth with her suburbs, and ____ with her suburbs" (1 Chronicles 6:73)
23. Notion
25. "The ____ of Kish Saul's father were lost" (1 Samuel 9:3)
27. Sighing sound
29. Preposition
30. "The friendship of the world is ____ with God" (James 4:4)
32. Volume
33. Father of Gaal (Judges 9:30)
35. Note on diatonic scale
38. ____ passant (chess term)

39. "If any man ____ to be first, the same shall be last" (Mark 9:35)
41. "Pray for them which despitefully ____ you" (Luke 6:28)
42. Swabs
46. To reward
47. Barter
50. Once more
51. "Behold, the nations are as a ____ of a bucket" (Isaiah 40:15)
52. All ____ (attentive)
53. Pitch
56. Baseball player (abbr.)
57. Like alt.
58. Laughing sound
59. Quadrant in D.C.

PUZZLE 25

Evelyn M. Boyington

ACROSS

1. Hoover, for example
4. "And I saw, and behold a white ____" (Revelation 6:2)
9. Auction action
12. "Beware of him, and ____ his voice" (Exodus 23:21)
14. "They gave him vinegar to drink mingled with ____" (Matthew 27:34)
15. Shoshonean tribe member
16. Scrambled scuffle
18. "And the Avims which dwelt in ____" (Deuteronomy 2:23)
20. Of considerable size
22. What a raconteur weaves?
23. "And in the fourth chariot ____ and bay horses" (Zechariah 6:3)
26. Cave dweller
27. Partner of rave
28. What Hebron was formerly called, and its namesakes (var., Genesis 35:27)
30. Preposition
32. ____ white
33. Bypass
34. Queen, for example
35. The royal ____
36. Teams
37. Melted, as a fuse
38. Deface
39. Bees in the bonnet?
41. One husband of Abigail
43. "Let the wicked fall into their own ____" (Psalm 141:10)
44. "God hath blessed thee ____" (two words, Psalm 45:2)
46. Aeries
49. "Manasseh made Judah and the inhabitants of Jerusalem to ____" (2 Chronicles 33:9)
50. "Unto Shem also, the father of all the children of ____" (Genesis 10:21)
52. Holding a grudge
53. ____ station
54. Packs away
55. Tatami (floor ____)

DOWN

1. Title of respect in Brazil and Portugal
2. Lincoln, to his nearest and dearest
3. "As when the ____ fire burneth" (Isaiah 64:2)
5. "Sihon king of the Amorites, and ____ king of Bashan" (Psalm 135:11)
6. Stadium sound
7. Smite
8. "____ the ninth" (1 Chronicles 12:12)
9. Charred
10. Inflammation (suffix)
11. Political partisan (abbr.)
13. Leaven
17. Building extension
19. Ages

21. "Entreat me not to ____ thee" (Ruth 1:16)
23. "The tree____, and was strong" (Daniel 4:11)
24. "Why do the heathen ____" (Psalm 2:1)
25. Overcome with noise
29. Shaggy mammals
30. ____ there, done that
31. Coniferous trees
33. Achieves success
34. "Their root shall be as rottenness, and their ____ shall go up as dust" (Isaiah 5:24)
36. Bat's bailiwick
37. Pierces

38. "In the resurrection they neither ____, nor are given in marriage" (Matthew 22:30)
40. "Your father hath. . . changed my wages ____ times" (Genesis 31:7)
41. Feminine name
42. "The reward not reckoned of grace, but of ____" (Romans 4:4)
44. Handful
45. Automobile of a previous generation
47. Singing syllable
48. Jelled
51. Inits. accorded a member of the clergy

PUZZLE 26

Evelyn M. Boyington

ACROSS

1. With Deborah, he confronted the army of Sisera (Judges 4)
5. One of the sons of Merari (1 Chronicles 6:30)
12. Poems
14. Burn with anger
15. Contented comment
17. "And the Lord God caused a ____ sleep" (Genesis 2:21)
19. "Suffer the little children to come unto ____" (Mark 10:14)
20. Apiece (abbr.)
21. Perimeter
23. Farm implements
25. The ____ Pavilions (Kaye novel)
26. Son of Seth
28. "I took the little book. . . and ____ it up" (Revelation 10:10)
29. In the ____
30. Information
32. Balmy state (abbr.)
33. Spanish pronoun
35. "In the ____ God created" (Genesis 1:1)
37. Exclamation of surprise
39. Concerning, with "in"
40. Oppressed person
42. "I. . .was come nigh unto Damascus about ____" (Acts 22:6)
44. "The Lord that delivered me out of the ____ of the lion" (1 Samuel 17:37)
46. "Thou art not a ____ of the law, but a judge" (James 4:11)
48. "For the stone shall ____ out of the wall" (Habakkuk 2:11)
49. Mentions
51. Bide a ____ (Scottish phrase)
52. Printer's measure
53. Great Commission verb
54. "The first came out red, . . . and they called his name ____" (Genesis 25:25)
56. Note on the diatonic scale
57. Abandon
60. "____ ye from your evil ways" (2 Kings 17:13)
62. "God. . .who hath called us unto his ____ glory by Christ Jesus" (1 Peter 5:10)
63. Daniel's den mates

DOWN

1. Announce loudly
2. Right page (abbr.)
3. "Which of you. . .can ____ one cubit unto his stature?" (Matthew 6:27)
4. "If ye love me, ____ my commandments" (John 14:15)
6. Resident of the Far East (abbr.)
7. Certain rocks
8. Command to a horse
9. With ____
10. "Then I will give them ____ ____ to know Me" (2 words, Jeremiah 24:7, NKJV)
11. "____ unto me: I will teach you the fear of the Lord" (Psalm 34:11)
13. Actress Ward

16. "Naphtali is a ____ let loose" (Genesis 49:21)
18. "The blessed and only____, the King of kings" (1 Timothy 6:15)
22. Ruth and Orpah were "women of ____" (Ruth 1:4)
24. Pronoun
25. Note on the diatonic scale
27. Cheerless
29. Ate out
31. "Strong meat belongeth to them that are of full ____" (Hebrews 5:14)
32. Old-fashioned hand towel message
34. Yield
36. Mature
38. "Moreover the Lord thy God will send the ____ among them" (Deuteronomy 7:20)
41. "My ____ did not slip" (Psalm 18:36)
43. Worried exclamation
44. Greek letter
45. Occident
47. Bridle part
49. ____ fields (what Jesus went through on the sabbath day, Mark 2:23)
50. Son of Kish
53. European tongue (abbr.)
55. Father of Bezaleel (Exodus 31:2)
58. Quadrant in D.C.
59. British 'bye
61. "And Abram said unto Lot, Let there be ____ strife" (Genesis 13:8)

PUZZLE 27

Evelyn M. Boyington

ACROSS

1. Member of Congress (abbr.)
4. "Behold, ____ ____ is in thine own eye" (2 words, Matthew 7:4)
9. Scheduled stopping place (abbr.)
12. Poetic preposition
13. "I will ____ thee seven years" (Genesis 29:18)
14. Handle roughly
15. "There is a friend that sticketh closer than a ____" (Proverbs 18:24)
17. Part of a book
19. Coop comment?
20. Nicholas, for one
21. "The children of Giddel, the children of ____" (Ezra 2:47)
23. "O thou ____ among women" (Song of Solomon 6:1)
26. Excuse me!
27. "Ehud the son of ____, a Benjamite" (Judges 3:15)
28. Preposition
29. Measure of Everest (abbr.)
30. "This is ___, which was for to come" (Matthew 11:14)
31. "With the ____ of an ass have I slain a thousand men" (Judges 15:16)
32. Continent (abbr.)
33. Nonsense (Brit.)
34. Table or pike
35. "He. . .shall be called the Son of the ___" (Luke 1:32)
38. "The birds of the air have ____" (Matthew 8:20)
39. Towel identification
40. Horned mammal
41. Describing a taskmaster
43. "A man of ____" (Isaiah's description of the Messiah)
46. Long, long time
47. "The sons of Shemidah were. . .Likhi, and ____" (1 Chronicles 7:19)
49. Greek form of Noah
50. You're all____!
51. House of ____
52. Compass pt.

DOWN

1. "Will a man ____ God?" (Malachi 3:8)
2. Always (poet.)
3. "That a great ____ is risen up among us" (Luke 7:16)
4. One of the twelve tribes of Israel
5. Horn holler?
6. "Ye do ____, not knowing the scriptures" (Matthew 22:29)
7. Thoroughfare (abbr.)
8. "We have found the ____" (John 1:41)
9. Steeple
10. More than freckled
11. "Stand in ___, and sin not" (Psalm 4:4)

16. Five make one in b'ball
18. Average
20. Stopover on the journey from Egypt to Jordan (Numbers 33:27)
21. Where Joshua was buried: "on the north side of the hill ____" (Judges 2:9)
22. "And the children of Sheshan; ____" (1 Chronicles 2:31)
23. Small, snappish dog
24. Maze instruction
25. Boroughs
27. To cover up
30. "He became the author of ____ salvation" (Hebrews 5:9)
31. "They have slain them which showed before of the coming of the ____ ____" (2 words, Acts 7:52)
34. Rend
36. Belgian city
37. Pronoun
38. Standards
40. Pester continuously
41. "A time to rend, and a time to ____" (Ecclesiastes 3:7)
42. What a "piggy" is
43. Title of respect
44. "A brother offended is harder to be ____ than a strong city" (Proverbs 18:19)
45. Understand
48. Favorite first word

PUZZLE 28

Evelyn M. Boyington

ACROSS

1. To engrave with acid
4. Common contraction
7. Woodwind
11. Powerful lobby in D.C.
12. Erstwhile emerald?
14. "_____ we like sheep have gone astray" (Isaiah 53:6)
15. Proximal's polar opposite
17. Central African nation
19. Gemstone comprising third foundation of wall of the New Jerusalem (Revelation 21:19)
21. To know (Scot.)
22. Spigot
24. Balaam's beast
25. Marble for marbles?
29. Scold constantly
31. "_____ is finished" (John 19:30)
32. Gem in second row of high priest's breastplate (Exodus 28:18)
33. "I find _____ fault in him" (John 19:4)
34. "And on earth peace, good will toward _____" (Luke 2:14)
36. Bottom of the barrel?
37. "Some of them thought, because Judas had the _____" (John 13:29)
38. Familiar name of Brazilian port
40. Geographical abbr.

42. Gemstone comprising seventh foundation of wall of 19 across
47. Return to original speed (music)
49. Indian communal village
51. Zilch
52. Formerly known as the coney, in Bible times
54. Row
55. Gem in fourth row of 32 across
56. "Thou anointest my head with _____" (Psalm 23:5)
57. Cause disintegration of blood cells

DOWN

1. "But the _____ of all things is at hand" (1 Peter 4:7)
2. Practical joker
3. Converts into cold, hard currency
4. Soft mineral
5. Linking verb
6. To scatter or cluster
7. Tree found on Persian Gulf
9. Not a spring chicken
10. Character actor Jack, whose stock-in-trade was westerns
12. Cohort
13. Conscious self
16. Exposure in Ixtapa?
18. "Go to the _____, thou sluggard" (Proverbs 6:6)
20. Covers with a hard, glossy surface
23. Slender cigars

24. Aspire to
25. First ____
26. Needlefish
27. What to wear
28. Printer's measures
30. ____ and Magog
    (Revelation 20:8)
35. Well
37. Young Yankee employee?
39. Measure of resistance
40. Sodium hydroxide
41. One billionth (prefix)
43. Measure of rotations (abbr.)
44. Toy or turkey?
45. Gemstone
46. Light (Lat.)
48. ____ ear

50. Mineral resource
53. Eastern seaboard state
    (abbr.)

PUZZLE 29

John H. Thornberg

ACROSS

1. Bashful
4. "Lest thou ____ thy foot against a stone" (Psalm 91:12)
8. "A glorious church, not having ____, or wrinkle" (Ephesians 5:27)
12. Sheltered from wind
13. Gnawing pain
14. Father of Ham, Shem, and Japheth
15. State that is bordered by Illinois (abbr.)
16. "Jesus saith unto them, Come and ____" (John 21:12)
17. Cattle or farm
18. Worship
20. Body parts between the waist and the knees
21. Ironic
22. Engage beforehand
25. Hard fat found in cattle and sheep
27. "The wisdom that is from above is. . .full of ____ and good fruits" (James 3:17)
28. Affirmative in Acapulco
29. "Your ____ men shall dream dreams" (Joel 2:28)
30. God worshiped by Jezebel, and its namesakes
31. Cotton ____
32. Article
33. Second planet from the sun
34. Small, headless nail

35. Qualities of a bishop: "____, not a brawler" (1 Timothy 3:3)
37. Command to a horse
38. Killer whale
39. One foundation of Christian life
42. "O ye of little ____" (Matthew 8:26)
44. City in Normandy
45. Command word
46. Big blunder
47. "That ye ____ one another" (John 13:34)
48. United
49. Preposition
50. If any man hear my voice, and ____ the door" (Revelation 3:20)
51. "That they may be ____, even as we are" (John 17:22)

DOWN

1. Make a mistake
2. "He that hath ears to ____" (Matthew 11:15)
3. Biblical pronoun
4. Jay's love in The Great Gatsby
5. Teen trauma
6. Pronoun
7. "Greater is ____ that is in you" (1 John 4:4)
8. Brisk and lively
9. Composure
10. Canoe component
11. "Hallowed be ____ name" (Matthew 6:9)
16. "Whose waters cast up mire and ____" (Isaiah 57:20)

17. Floppy ones?
19. Astonished
20. Feathered fishing lures
22. Real winner (colloq.)
23. Encompassing the Orient
24. "Charity suffereth long, and is ____" (1 Corinthians 13:4)
25. "For though thou wash thee with nitre, and take thee much____" (Jeremiah 2:22)
26. Bone of the forearm
27. Bread from heaven
30. Hardwood tree
31. "The beauty of old men is the ____ head" (Proverbs 20:29,var.)
33. "Add to your faith ____" (2 Peter 1:5)
34. Noggin

36. What the bread winner must do
37. "But her leaf shall be ____" (Jeremiah 17:8)
39. ____ the way
40. First home
41. "And he ____ upon a cherub, and did fly" (Psalm 18:10)
42. Airport abbr.
43. Vowel trio
44. To go back on a promise, with "out"
47. Biblical exclamation
48. Officer of the U.S. Army (abbr.)

PUZZLE 30

John H. Thornberg

ACROSS

1. Shushan, per the NIV
5. ____ cake
9. "I therefore so ____, not as uncertainly; so fight I" (1 Corinthians 9:26)
12. Tore
13. The Syrians of ____ (2 Samuel 10:6, hired by Ammon's heirs to fight David)
14. "Love ____ another" (1 John 4:7)
15. Brother of Jacob
16. Brother of Cain
17. Fuss
18. History
20. Moses' mouthpiece
22. Friendship
25. Alto ____ (jazz instrument)
26. O.T. major prophet (abbr.)
27. Melchizedek, king of ____
30. "O sole ___ "
33. Seth's sire
34. Bridle part
35. Together
36. Time of revival (abbr.)
37. "City of David" (Luke 2:4)
39. What CBS, for one, would like to do: ___Fox?
40. Elemental particles
41. Shake violently
44. Window component
46. Crone
47. Like a funk

49. N.T. book
53. "Love worketh no ____ to his neighbour" (Romans 13:10)
54. Like a certain "ranger"
55. "But ____ found grace in the eyes of the Lord" (Genesis 6:8)
56. Two-____, as tissue
57. Loose ____
58. Times long past

DOWN

1. Compass dir.
2. Moments of elation
3. "Let the ____ roar, and the fulness thereof" (Psalm 96:11)
4. One who votes
5. Peter, for one
6. "And they put on him a purple ____" (John 19:2)
7. Honest one
8. Son of Beor (Numbers 22:5)
9. Deafening din
10. Let go
11. ____ tetra (tropical fish)
19. Yiddish exclamations
21. Get rid of
22. Slightly open
23. Darius the ____ (Daniel 11:1)
24. Middle Eastern country
25. Father of Enos (Luke 3:38)
28. Be a party to
29. American ____ (college course, abbr.)

30. Line that separates the earth's crust from its mantle (abbr.)
31. Thing to be done
32. Units of electrical resistance
35. City near Jerusalem
37. Collection
38. _____ Cruces, NM
39. Conjunction
41. Single snack
42. "Then led they Jesus. . . unto the _____ of judgment" (John 18:28)
43. Unsightly
44. "Here am I; _____ me" (Isaiah 6:8)

45. Mimics
48. Many moons
50. Dove ditty
51. Bituminous pitch
52. Pronoun

PUZZLE 31

Janet W. Adkins

ACROSS

1. Great amount
5. Lea denizen
8. "All _____ that we should be saved was. . .taken away" (Acts 27:20)
12. Son of Joah (1 Chronicles 6:21)
13. Gold, in Guatanamo
14. Grandson of Adam
15. "Neither count I my life_____ unto myself" (Acts 20:24)
16. Bled, as fabric
17. Used to be
18. Usually 15 percent
20. To _____ for
22. Father of Rachel, and his namesakes
25. Cause great anger
29. Author of Tristram Shandy
30. 911 happy ending
31. Naval officer (abbr.)
32. Laughing syllable
33. "Make a great flame with smoke _____ _____ out of the city" (2 words, Judges 20:38)
37. Belonging to the first son of Eliphaz (Genesis 36:11)
41. "We who are Jews by _____" (Galatians 2:15)
42. "_____ _____ Abana and Pharpar. . .better than all the waters of Israel?" (2 Kings 5:12)
43. Number of performances of a play
44. Day _____
45. Get out of
48. Former Mideast republic (abbr.)
50. Feminine name
54. "When ye _____ the harvest of your land" (Leviticus 23:22)
55. Hwy.
56. She was called "tender eyed"
57. Feminine name
58. Still
59. Writer Bombeck

DOWN

1. "I will _____ evil beasts out of the land" (Leviticus 26:6)
2. Netherlands metropolis
3. Feminine name
4. _____ board
5. "They came and took up his _____, and laid it in a tomb" (Mark 6:29)
6. Mouth (pl.)
7. "And there appeared another _____ in heaven" (Revelation 12:3)
8. "Let them live; but let them be _____ of wood" (Joshua 9:21)
9. Holy _____ of Israel
10. _____ favor (Sp.)
11. Compass pt.
19. "There was no room for them in the _____" (Luke 2:7)

21. Chemical suffix
22. Place of the seal (abbr.)
23. Entrance court (pl.)
24. Untamed one
26. Son of Carmi who was stoned by all of Israel (Joshua 7)
27. Fertilizer from sea birds
28. Shoe width
33. Hosp. employee
34. Continent which includes Italia
35. S.A. country
36. "But the talk of the lips tendeth only to ____" (Proverbs 14:23)
37. Musical instrument of the Old Testament (Isaiah 5:12)
38. Rather than
39. "____ not with him that flattereth with his lips" (Proverbs 20:19)
40. Elm, for one (abbr.)
45. Eastern state univ.
46. Uncle of Saul (1 Samuel 14:50)
47. Plug up
49. Consumed
51. Poetic preposition
52. Candidate for a burnt offering
53. Exclamation

PUZZLE 32

Janet W. Adkins

ACROSS

1. Rouen repository
5. Douglas, for one
8. Father of Gaal
   (Judges 9:26)
12. Zest
13. Act or process (suffix)
14. "If a man ____ me, he will
    keep my words"
    (John 14:23)
15. City in western Germany
16. "Peter, . . .____ unto the
    sepulchre" (Luke 24:12)
17. Paradise
18. "There shall not be found
    among you. . .a charmer, . . .
    or a ____"
    (Deuteronomy 18:10–11)
21. Lend an ____
22. Witticism
23. Maximum
26. "Trust in the Lord, . . .and
    verily thou shalt be ____"
    (Psalm 37:3)
27. "A brother offended is
    harder to be ____ than a
    strong city" (Proverbs 18:19)
30. He was (Lat.)
31. ____ pottage (dish served in
    Genesis 25:30)
32. "And Judah and Israel
    dwelt safely, . . .under his
    ____" (1 Kings 4:25)
33. Paving material
34. "A golden bell and a pome-
    granate, upon the ____ of
    the robe" (Exodus 28:34)
35. With fewer impurities
36. Son of Noah
    (var., Luke 3:36)
37. Wrongdoing
38. "He found them ten times
    better than all the. . .____"
    (Daniel 1:20)
43. On a cruise
44. Mini____
45. Pester
47. "God sent him forth from
    the garden. . .to ____ the
    ground" (Genesis 3:23)
48. Work unit
49. Server's advantage,
    in tennis
50. Unbelievable, as a story
51. Dentist's degree (abbr.)
52. Two nonconsecutive notes
    on the diatonic scale

DOWN

1. Community consumer org.
2. Elvis' middle name
3. Number of holes on a par-
   three course, usually
4. "Lest he be wise in his own
   ____" (Proverbs 26:5)
5. Hubbub
6. Last duke from the line of
   Esau (Genesis 36:43)
7. Appointed another
   appellation
8. "And I will bring forth a
   seed. . .and mine ____ shall
   inherit it" (Isaiah 65:9)
9. Augur
10. At any time
11. Where thieves dwell?
19. Tattle, with "on"
20. Where Cain dwelt

(Genesis 4:16)

23. Rent out
24. Masculine name
25. Spoil
26. Not masc.
27. "I count all things but loss. . . that I may _____ Christ" (Philippians 3:8)
28. "When we are absent _____ from another" (Genesis 31:49)
29. Father of Abner (2 Samuel 3:23)
31. Separated
32. "Come thou hither, . . .and dip thy morsel in the _____" (Ruth 2:14)
34. "Walk about Zion, and go round about _____"

(Psalm 48:12)

35. "They sewed _____ leaves together" (Genesis 3:7)
36. Hesitate
37. "Thou shalt compass me about with _____ of deliverance" (Psalm 32:7)
38. Continent
39. Mimic a merchant
40. Ingredient definitely not found in low-fat recipes
41. Sat high in the saddle
42. "For Paul had determined to _____ by Ephesus" (Acts 20:16)
43. Corporate giant (abbr.)
46. Genetic material

PUZZLE 33

Janet W. Adkins

ACROSS

1. Ancient Hebrew dry measure (pl.)
5. Fifteenth division of Psalm 119
7. Snare to trap game or fish
8. "And Samuel told him every ____" (1 Samuel 3:18)
10. Weak day? (abbr.)
11. "I am ____ at my very heart" (Jeremiah 4:19)
13. "Lucifer, ____ of the morning! how art thou cut down to the ground" (Isaiah 14:12)
14. "Speakest to ____ the wicked from his wicked way" (Ezekiel 3:18)
15. "La ____" (Debussy composition)
17. Omen; portent
19. Withhold nothing
21. Pronoun
22. Black ____
23. Pronoun for a seaworthy vessel
24. U.S. West Indies territory (abbr.)
25. "And David heard. . .that ____ did shear his sheep" (1 Samuel 25:4)
27. Knight's steed
29. O.T. book (abbr.)
30. Chinese canine breed
31. Age

32. Lot, to Abraham
34. Foot or footlike structure (zool.)
35. Fencer's gear
36. ____ France
37. "I am like an owl of the ____" (Psalm 102:6)
39. "And the veil of the temple was ____ in twain" (Mark 15:38)

DOWN

1. Give a pink slip
2. "____ I my brother's keeper?" (Genesis 4:9)
3. "____ of the leaven of the Pharisees" (Matthew 16:6)
4. Twenty-first division of Psalm 119
5. "If thou doest not well, ____ lieth at the door" (Genesis 4:7)
6. Liquid measure of ancient Hebrews
7. All ____!
9. To make suitable
10. Like all humans
11. This may be flipped
12. God (Lat.)
13. "They toil not, neither do they ____" (Matthew 6:28)
14. "Son of man, ____ for the multitude of Egypt" (Ezekiel 32:18)
16. "All the ____ run into the sea" (Ecclesiastes 1:7)
18. One who is warded off?
19. Author of Pygmalion

20. Money, in Milano
23. Demonstrate
26. David _____ Gurion
27. Stilton, for one
28. Late actor Will
30. "Be of good _____"
    (Matthew 9:2)
33. Catalog abbr.
34. "I am counted with them
    that go down into the _____"
    (Psalm 88:4)
36. Masculine nickname
38. Printer's measure

PUZZLE 34

Janet W. Adkins

ACROSS

1. Diva's defining moment
5. One who comes out, familiarly
8. Land measure
12. Preceding portrait or pity?
13. Mist (Scot.)
14. What every word in the Bible is
15. American playwright
16. Stadium sound
17. Actress Daly
18. Imitate
20. Linking verb
22. Birthplace of Saul
25. "The Lord knoweth the thoughts of man, that they are _____" (Psalm 94:11)
29. "In Damascus the governor under _____ the king" (2 Corinthians 11:32)
30. "For how can I _____ to see the evil that shall come unto my people?" (Esther 8:6)
31. Wrongly (prefix)
32. Twelve-step gp.
33. "In lowliness of mind let each _____ other better than themselves" (Philippians 2:3)
37. French painter Pierre Auguste _____
41. "_____ my soul from their destructions" (Psalm 35:17)
42. "Ye were without Christ, being _____ from the commonwealth of Israel" (Ephesians 2:12)
43. Vacuum tube (abbr.)
44. Father of Saul, king of Israel
45. He offered "a more excellent sacrifice" than his brother
48. Exclamation of disbelief
50. Prophetess who awaited the Messiah
54. Used to be
55. Before (poet.)
56. "For thou art a _____ kinsman" (Ruth 3:9)
57. Corn quantity (pl.)
58. N.T. book (abbr.)
59. May be

DOWN

1. He succeeded his father, King Abijam (1 Kings 15:8)
2. Area (abbr.)
3. _____ de la Cite, in Paris
4. "But when thou makest _____ _____, call the poor, the maimed" (2 words, Luke 14:13)
5. Use of force or threats
6. Historical period
7. "Let us _____ ourselves valiantly for our people" (1 Chronicles 19:13)
8. Wait on
9. Wail
10. String of victories
11. Shoe width
19. "Of _____, the family of the Punites" (Numbers 26:23)
21. Sprinted
22. Less spicy

23. Bail out of bed
24. Musical notations
26. Measures used worldwide (abbr.)
27. "____ up a child in the way he should go" (Proverbs 22:6)
28. Parts of a century
34. O.T. book. (abbr.)
35. Continent (abbr.)
36. ____-ammah, chief city of the Philistines (2 Samuel 8:1)
37. Jacob served Laban fourteen years for her
38. Father of Hophni and Phineas
39. Belonging to the first month, the month in which Pur was cast (Esther 3:7)
40. Whirlwind near the Faeroe Islands
45. "Stand in ____, and sin not" (Psalm 4:4)
46. Aunt ____ of TV's Mayberry
47. "To ____ is human"
49. Son of Jether (1 Chronicles 7:38)
51. Born (Fr.)
52. Not (Scot.)
53. "Thou hast scattered thine enemies with thy strong ____" (Psalm 89:10)

PUZZLE 35

Janet W. Adkins

ACROSS

1. Exclamation of sorrow
5. Catalog promise (abbr.)
8. "But ____ found grace in the eyes of the Lord" (Genesis 6:8)
12. Greek form of feminine name that means "princess"
13. ____ wife
14. ____-Lebanon (mountain range in W. Syria, which includes Mt. Hermon)
15. Not ready to turn pro (abbr.)
16. Bone
17. Cave dwellers
18. New Testament epistle
22. The green, green grass of home?
23. ____ of the above
24. Like a sprinter
27. 1/1000th of an inch
28. Exodus character
31. "For ____ be called, but few chosen" (Matthew 20:16)
32. Prevent
33. "Diana. . .should be destroyed, whom all ____. . . worshippeth" (Acts 19:27)
34. Employ
35. Biblical verb
36. "Let us ____ before the Lord our maker" (Psalm 95:6)
37. Greek letter
38. "And the ____ gave up the dead which were in it" (Revelation 20:13)
39. "The Lord hath given you the land, . . .all the ____. . . faint because of you" (Joshua 2:9)
44. Concept (comb. form)
45. Historical period
46. Tiny amount (colloq.)
48. Bereft; desolate (arch.)
49. Beam of light
50. Masculine name
51. Healing plant
52. Affirmative
53. "Simon ____. . ."

DOWN

1. Old Testament king whose name means "physician"
2. "For thou art my ____. . .the Lord will lighten my darkness" (2 Samuel 22:29)
3. Son of Ulla (1 Chronicles 7:39)
4. "O ____ us early with thy mercy" (Psalm 90:14)
5. Progenitor (colloq.)
6. With "down," way to meet the bed
7. "We are perplexed, but not in ____" (2 Corinthians 4:8)
8. Husband of Abigail (1 Samuel 25:3)
9. Second son of Judah (1 Chronicles 2:3)
10. Members of the bar (abbr.)
11. Possessive pronoun

19. His wife turned into a pillar of salt
20. Part of the psyche
21. Under the weather
24. Texas institute of higher learning (abbr.)
25. Had been
26. Suffix used to form feminine nouns
27. Welcome ____
28. Enzyme of vegetable origin (suffix)
29. Grain mentioned in the Old Testament (Isaiah 28:25)
30. Suitable for (suffix)
32. "And fire shall consume the tabernacles of ____" (Job 15:34)
33. Husband of Sapphira
35. "And there was war between ____ and Baasha king of Israel" (1 Kings 15:16)
36. Greek island in the Aegean
37. Single speech sound
38. Corset (Brit.)
39. Matinee ____
40. Notorious emperor of Rome
41. *Dies* ___
42. Brother of Job (Genesis 46:13)
43. Don't leave!
44. Longshoremen's org.
47. Solution (abbr.)

PUZZLE 36

Janet W. Adkins

ACROSS

1. Don't just sit there
4. "I do ____ my bow in the cloud" (Genesis 9:13)
7. Mightier than a machete?
10. Vast desert region (abbr.)
11. Of a certain Indochinese kingdom
12. Enthusiasm
13. "For whom he did fore-know, he also did ____" (Romans 8:29)
16. "Wound for wound, ____ for ____" (clue repeated) (Exodus 21:25)
17. Drunkard
18. Shows or does (suffix)
19. Epitome of wisdom
23. ____ au lait
25. Chums
26. Corrida cheer
27. "They lavish gold. . .hire a goldsmith; and he maketh it ____ ____" (2 words, Isaiah 46:6)
28. "They of Persia and of ____ . . .were in thine army" (Ezekiel 27:10)
29. ____ code
30. "Lest I ____ mine own inheritance" (Ruth 4:6)
31. Ancient meeting place, in a city
32. Organ component
33. Omen
35. The Great ____
36. Half of 104, to Hadrian
37. "Ye were ____ with that holy Spirit of promise" (Ephesians 1:13)
40. "Ye are complete in him, which is the head of all ____ and power" (Colossians 2:10)
43. Helps
44. College entrance requirement (abbr.)
45. Three, in Turin
46. Not (Scot.)
47. Atlas, for one (abbr., pl.)
48. Well-spoken affirmative

DOWN

1. Cleopatra's instrument of death, and others
2. "They laid the ark of the Lord upon the ____" (1 Samuel 6:11)
3. "____ shall a man leave his father and his mother" (Genesis 2:24)
4. Drifted off
5. "Rise up, ye women that are at ____" (Isaiah 32:9)
6. Young one
7. Greek philosopher
8. Put on the feedbag
9. Compass dir.
12. Certain chemical compounds
14. Went out on the town
15. Tristran and ____, of the medieval legend
19. Prepare certain dishes

20. "For we. . .do groan, . . .that
    _____ might be swallowed up
    of life" (2 Corinthians 5:4)
21. Oil (comb. form)
22. _____ tide
23. Become one with nature?
24. "For this _____ is mount
    Sinai in Arabia"
    (Galatians 4:25)
25. Of a sandy beach
29. "Set me as _____ _____ upon
    thine heart" (2 words, Song
    of Solomon 8:6)
31. "When her masters saw that
    the hope of their _____ was
    gone" (Acts 16:19)
34. Playground perennial

35. "Ye love the uppermost
    _____ in the synagogues"
    (Luke 11:43)
37. "He _____ on the ground,
    and made clay" (John 9:6)
38. To be (Fr.)
39. Colors
40. _____ fried
41. Long, narrow inlet
42. Doctrine or theory
    (Suffix)

PUZZLE 37

Janet W. Adkins

ACROSS

1. Once more; again
5. Egyptian cobra, for one
8. "Launch out. . .let down your ____ for a draught" (Luke 5:4)
12. Feminine nickname (var.)
13. 1/1000th of an inch
14. "____, lama sabachthani?" (Mark 15:34)
15. With "off," visibly upset
16. Defined time of history
17. Bobbin of a weaver's shuttle
18. Have
20. U.S. medical research org.
22. Woman married (two words)
25. "The Lord is thy ____: . . . thy shade upon thy right hand" (Psalm 121:5)
29. Doesn't pedal
30. "But to him that ____ righteousness shall be a sure reward" (Proverbs 11:18)
31. Assn.
32. Definite article
33. Depended upon
37. "____, which had kept his bed eight years, and was sick of the palsy" (Acts 9:33)
40. What the frontrunner will do
41. One of "the seven churches in Asia" (Revelation 1:11)
42. Long, undetermined time

43. Son of Noah (var., Luke 3:36)
44. Having to do with the community (abbr.)
47. Anger
49. Wood for a funeral rite
53. "____ was a great man among the Anakims" (Joshua 14:15)
55. Corn serving
56. "Not one ____ of his head fall to the ground" (1 Samuel 14:45)
57. Gossip (colloq.)
58. Promotion for a police officer (abbr.)
59. They attend Promise Keepers events

DOWN

1. Corporate giant (abbr.)
2. Jacqueline Kennedy, ____ Bouvier
3. Before (poet.)
4. "But the younger ____ refuse: . . .they will marry" (1 Timothy 5:11)
5. Make ____
6. Title of respect
7. "So Solomon. . .covered the floor of the house with ____ of fir" (1 Kings 6:14–15)
8. "He shall neither have son nor ____ among his people" (Job 18:19)
9. High priest who raised Samuel

10. High, rocky hill
11. Wrongdoing
19. ____ paint
21. Vowel trio
22. Prepare meat for grilling
23. One of the fenced cities of Naphtali (Joshua 19:38)
24. "Though thou shouldest make thy nest as high as the ____" (Jeremiah 49:16)
26. His name literally means "a stone"
27. Leader Allen of the Green Mountain Boys
28. Father of Joanna (Luke 3:27)
34. Wrath
35. Part of the psyche

36. "The cock shall not crow, till thou hast ____ me thrice" (John 13:38)
37. Express one's opinion
38. Crony (arch.)
39. Maiden in mythology
44. Possessed with a devil
45. Eastern state univ.
46. Where an inch is really an inch (abbr.)
48. Feminine name
50. Sweet potato
51. Grain mentioned in the Old Testament (Isaiah 28:25)
52. Sea eagle
54. "Then said I, ____ ,Lord God" (Jeremiah 1:6)

PUZZLE 38

Janet W. Adkins

ACROSS

1. _____ water
4. One of Shem's children (Genesis 10:22)
8. Business correspondence abbr.
12. That (Sp.)
13. Latvian monetary unit
14. Composer Stravinsky
15. Becoming slower, in music (abbr.)
16. Layer
17. _____ of the above
18. "_____ not at the matter: for he that is higher. . . regardeth" (Ecclesiastes 5:8)
20. _____ culpa
22. Person concerned with (suffix)
23. Evergreen tree of the cypress family, known for its berries
27. "Thou shalt be missed, because thy _____ will be empty" (1 Samuel 20:18)
29. Source of poi
30. Norma _____, Oscar-winning movie
31. "So Manasseh made Judah and the inhabitants of Jerusalem to _____" (2 Chronicles 33:9)
32. "So will I do for my servants' _____, that I may not destroy them all" (Isaiah 65:8)
33. Carbohydrate (suffix)

34. Resinous substance of South Asia
35. Canned (colloq.)
36. Not brand new
37. Son of Uzziah (Nehemiah 11:4)
39. One (Scot.)
40. Mountain stat.
41. "He is _____ of death" (Matthew 26:66)
44. He helped build the towns of Ono and Lod (1 Chronicles 8:12)
47. Steel beam used in construction
49. Biblical exclamation
50. Presidential power
51. Alley Oop's girlfriend
52. Paving substance
53. "The land is as the garden of _____ before them" (Joel 2:3)
54. Joyeux _____ (holiday greetings in Grenoble?)
55. Sea eagle

DOWN

1. Time in an elected office
2. "All they which dwelt in _____ heard the word of the Lord Jesus" (Acts 19:10)
3. "Let me freely speak unto you of the _____ David" (Acts 2:29)
4. Amend slightly
5. Complain bitterly
6. Gobbled up
7. "But their scribes and Pharisees _____ against his disciples" (Luke 5:30)

8. _____ Peninsula
9. Time past
10. "Unto us a child is born, unto us a _____ is given" (Isaiah 9:6)
11. Before (poet.)
19. Profession of the late James Herriot (colloq.)
21. Son of Seth
23. Father of Agur (Proverbs 30:1)
24. "Woe unto you, scribes and Pharisees, . . .ye compass sea and land to make one _____" (Matthew 23:15)
25. At _____ (heard at boot camp)
26. Bane of oboist?
27. Actress Ward
28. He was (Lat.)

29. "He exacted the silver and. . . gold. . .of every one according to his _____" (2 Kings 23:35)
32. Breeze along
36. Iowa institute of higher learning (abbr.)
38. "And Moses told _____ all the words of the Lord" (Exodus 4:28)
39. Related to the sense of hearing
41. Strong wind
42. Speed along
43. Seafarer's woolly tale?
44. Whom the serpent be____ ever so subtly
45. Hotel roo____
46. Sum____
48.

PUZZLE 39

Janet W. Adkins

ACROSS

1. And so on (abbr.)
4. Describing nonclergy
8. "This _____ Jesus, which is taken up from you into heaven" (Acts 1:11)
12. Gala event, to Gabrielle
13. _____ Domini
14. "The Lord be a _____ and faithful witness" (Jeremiah 42:5)
15. Poetic contraction
16. Welcome benefit or blessing
17. Transportation (colloq.)
18. "All the land of Canaan fainted by _____ of the famine" (Genesis 47:13)
20. "The children of Keros, the children of _____" (Nehemiah 7:47)
22. Uncle of Saul (1 Samuel 14:50)
23. Fortified rampart
27. Hit TV show
29. "And his _____ went throughout all Syria" (Matthew 4:24)
30. Busy one
31. U_____ as talent
33. _____ named Lazarus, _____ at his gate, _____ (Luke 16:20)

38. "I will utter dark _____ of old" (Psalm 78:2)
40. "Lord, if it be thou, _____ me come unto thee on the water" (Matthew 14:28)
41. The year 1501, to Flavius
42. Son of Levi (Numbers 3:17)
45. Continent
48. Change direction slightly
50. Land where Cain dwelt (Genesis 4:16)
51. What is unfurled
52. Fencing sword
53. Food fish
54. Actress Daly
55. Actress Talbott
56. WWII milieu (abbr.)

DOWN

1. Father of Peleg and Joktan (Genesis 10:25)
2. Noxious weed (Matthew 13)
3. "Create in me a _____ heart, O God" (Psalm 51:10)
4. Apply some elbow grease
5. Therefore (arch.)
6. Ending for many words in Italian
7. Devours
8. "She [Rebekah] said. . .We have both _____ and provender enough" (Genesis 24:25)
9. Onassis
10. Miry clay
11. Shoe width
19. "I will _____ no wicked thing before mine eyes" (Psalm 101:3)
21. The Philippines, for example, to Rene
22. Uncovers

24. "And he brought forth the spoil of the city in great ____" (2 Samuel 12:30)
25. Nevada city
26. "Thou wilt ____ him in perfect peace" (Isaiah 26:3)
27. Times of historical significance
28. "In ____ was there a voice heard, lamentation, and weeping" (Matthew 2:18)
29. "Be of good cheer; thy sins be ____ thee" (Matthew 9:2)
32. "After the ____ which they call heresy, so worship I the God" (Acts 24:14)
33. "A foolish man, which built his house upon the ____" (Matthew 7:26)

37. "In the night ____ of Moab is laid waste, and brought to silence" (Isaiah 15:1)
39. Another word for idol
40. City of Macedonia where Paul preached
42. "With them in the clouds, to ____ the Lord in the air" (1 Thessalonians 4:17)
43. "For he shall grow up. . .as a ____ out of a dry ground" (Isaiah 53:2)
44. "____ the seer" (2 Chronicles 12:15)
45. Rear of a ship
46. Cunning
47. John (Scot.)
49. On or upon (prefix)

PUZZLE 40

Janet W. Adkins

ACROSS

1. Juliette Low's organization (abbr.)
4. Depot (abbr.)
7. ____ reliever
11. "The ____ state of that man is worse than the first" (Luke 11:26)
13. Desire
14. Competent
15. Theory
16. Old auto
17. Wild goat
18. Stinging comment
19. Welfare; benefit
21. "And ____ also the Jairite was a chief ruler about David" (2 Samuel 20:26)
23. Part of a day (abbr.)
24. One-____ is a tithe
27. Righteous, symbolical name of Israel (var.)
32. One of Lamech's two wives (Genesis 4:19)
33. Conjunction
34. Late folk singer Laura
35. David's nephew (2 Samuel 13:3)
38. "Yet through the ____ of water it will bud, and bring forth boughs" (Job 14:9)
39. Certain therapist (abbr.)
40. Kitchen necessity
41. "Can two walk ____" (Amos 3:3)
46. "____ it Romantic?"
49. Inter ____
50. On or upon (prefix)
51. Ocean Sciences (abbr.)
52. Practices fabrication
53. ____ Perce, North American Indian tribe
54. Heads
56. Center; source
57. Understand; realize
58. "____ unto you, scribes and Pharisees" (Matthew 23:14)

DOWN

1. Speaking too easily
2. Actress Thompson
3. Tribe to which Anna the prophetess belonged (Luke 2:36)
4. Mideast country
5. Problem child?
6. "And he [Samson] said. . . then shall I be weak, and be as ____ man" (Judges 16:11)
7. Matched set
8. French clergy member
9. Channel, Solomon, Hawaiian, et al., to Christophe
10. ____! (word heard in a queue)
12. Aka Dorcas (Acts 9:36)
20. Sounds of hesitation
22. ____ factor (group of antigens)
24. ____ Mahal
25. People living in southern Nigeria
26. Feminine nickname
27. Patient and faithful sufferer

28. "But ye have an _____ from the Holy One, and ye know all things" (1 John 2:20)
29. Deli loaf
30. Footed vase
31. _____ a chance
36. Period
37. Site of Mars' hill
38. Thus
40. "In a race run all, but one receiveth the _____" (1 Corinthians 9:24)
41. Bath powder
42. Highly spiced stew
43. The _____ eagle (fowl not to be eaten; Leviticus 11:18)
44. "Among these nations shalt thou find no _____"

(Deuteronomy 28:65)
45. Fencer's adjunct
47. Garbage _____
48. Mount _____, in the land of Moab, gateway to Canaan (Deuteronomy 32:49)
55. Compass point

PUZZLE 41

Janet W. Adkins

ACROSS

1. "For ____ have sinned, and come short of the glory of God" (Romans 3:23)
4. ____ Miner's Daughter (Loretta Lynn film biography)
8. ____ California
12. Misery
13. "He died unto sin ___: but in that he liveth" (Romans 6:10)
14. Son of Shobal (Genesis 36:23)
15. "Angels which kept not their first ____" (Jude 6)
17. In close proximity
19. "Kiss the Son, ____ he be angry, and ye perish" (Psalm 2:12)
21. Alaskan outpost
22. Extinct creatures
25. Upper ____
27. Calm; tranquil
28. Where Stephane keeps his savings
29. Young man
32. "Thou shalt dwell in the land of Goshen, and thou shalt ____ ____ unto me" (2 words, Genesis 45:10)
34. "Thy ____, O God, is for ever and ever" (Psalm 45:6)
36. What old colleges do?
37. Hand (Sp.)
39. The Thin Man's (of moviedom) best friend?
40. Simon ____
41. "____ ye in at the strait gate" (Matthew 7:13)
42. Son of Eliphaz (Genesis 36:11)
45. What crowed (Matthew 26:75)
47. "The governor under ____ the king kept the city of the Damascenes" (2 Corinthians 11:32)
49. One like Mr. Dithers (of the comics), and others
53. With 20 Down, singing syllables
54. First murder victim
56. Retirement acct.
57. Printer's measure
58. Darius the ____, ruler of Babylon
59. See ____

DOWN

1. "Stand in ___, and sin not" (Psalm 4:4)
2. ____ Alamos
3. "____ all the earth fear the Lord" (Psalm 33:8)
4. Shelters for farm animals
5. Individuals
6. Dog days demand (abbr.)
7. Where the cedars were acclaimed (abbr.)
8. "____ Buddies" (short-lived 80s TV sit-com)
9. City in southern Judah (Joshua 15:50)
10. Color of green
11. Church denomination (abbr.)
16. "He sitteth ____ and keepeth silence" (Lamentations 3:28)
18. He "walked with God"
20. With 53 Across, singing syllable

22. The reward not reckoned of grace, but of ____"
    (Romans 4:4)
23. Preposition
24. "If any man will come after me, let him ____ himself"
    (Matthew 16:24)
26. Aware of what's really happening (colloq.)
28. "Doth the wild ass ____ when he hath grass?"
    (Job 6:5)
29. "For the Son of man is come to save that which was ____" (Matthew 18:11)
30. To pay one's share (colloq.)
31. "Neither count I my life ____ unto myself"
    (Acts 20:24)
33. ____ Colonies, Iowa historic communities

35. Holds a certain position
38. Group that advises the President (abbr.)
40. God allowed him to harm Job
41. School (Fr.)
42. "We spend our years as a ____ that is told"
    (Psalm 90:9)
43. Head of the Eranites
    (Numbers 26:36)
44. Honey, in the pure, clarified form
46. Father of Jesse
48. Masculine nickname
50. Title of respect
51. Poetic contraction
52. Got the blues
55. "____ sober" (1 Peter 5:8)

PUZZLE 42

Janet W. Adkins

ACROSS

1. Rascal
4. Le Cote _____ (W. Africa region)
7. Son of Enoch (Genesis 4:18)
11. Woman was made from _____ _____ (2 words)
13. Her name means "life"
14. Spy (colloq.)
15. _____ de soie (rich, silken material)
16. Fall flower, for short
17. "A flattering mouth worketh _____" (Proverbs 26:28)
18. Of considerable size, as a drink
19. "And Israel dwelt in all the cities of the _____" (Numbers 21:25)
21. Used to be
23. WWII red-letter day (abbr.)
24. "A virtuous _____ is a crown to her husband" (Proverbs 12:4)
27. "And Saul smote the Amalekites from _____ until . . .Shur" (1 Samuel 15:7)
32. "And Israel. . .spread his tent beyond the tower of _____" (Genesis 35:21)
33. "Therefore God, . . .hath anointed thee with the _____ of gladness" (Psalm 45:7)
34. One conquered by Persia
35. Stringed instrument resembling a lyre, in the Bible
37. Aussie tennis great
38. And (Fr.)
39. _____ Harbor, NY
40. "Lest. . .when I have preached to others, I. . .should be a _____" (1 Corinthians 9:27)
45. _____ the Terrible, Russian czar
49. Ancient Hebrew dry measure
50. Broadcast
51. Mount _____, in the land of Moab (Deuteronomy 32:49)
52. Bill of fare
53. Louis XV, par exemple
54. First name in murder mysteries (and Perry's creator)
55. _____bellum South (period following Civil War)
56. Gov't. drug prevention org.
57. Affirmative

DOWN

1. Like Queeg or Bligh (abbr.)
2. _____ code
3. Popular soap
4. "Luke, the beloved physician, and _____, greet you" (Colossians 4:14)
5. Mature female cell
6. Dismissal
7. Son of Bani (1 Chronicles 9:4)
8. Defeat utterly
9. "When he speaketh _____ _____, he speaketh of his own" (2 words, John 8:44)

10. Cubs' "cribs"?
12. Fortress
20. N.T. book (abbr.)
22. Article
24. NBA great Unseld
25. Harem room
26. Son of (Scot., prefix)
27. Used physical force
28. "How long will ye _____ mischief against a man" (Psalm 62:3)
29. O.T. book (abbr.)
30. Summer drink
31. Pronoun
33. "For which cause we faint not; . . .though our _____ man perish" (2 Corinthians 4:16)

36. Feminine nickname
37. Calif. city
39. Mideast country
40. Unconscious condition
41. "So be it"
42. Faxed
43. Factual and actual
44. Vowel quartet
46. "Every thing that he had made, . . .was _____ good" (Genesis 1:31)
47. Skilled; competent
48. Greek form of father of Shem, and his namesakes

Bible Crossword Answers

PUZZLE 1

W	O	R	L	D	S		S	G
A	R	I	A		A	B	I		I	L	K	S

W O R L D S — S G
A R I A — A B I — I L K S
S A T I A T E D — M A S T
— E S T — H O S
M A S H — I N C E N S E D
I F — S T E A L — G O
C O — R A B B I — B Y
A R — S A L A — W E P T
H E A P — T O P H E T H
— M U L E — W E A R
D A M N A B L E — T A R E
E X O — L A I T Y — O R
W E N — A L P H A — E E

PUZZLE 2

E H I — O R P A H — M E
H E N — R O U S E — S A Y
U Z — T A B L E — H I D E
D E B A T E — R U I N E D
— K E R O S — S E A
W I S E R — K E L I T A
E A T — A B S — O R
T H I R S T Y — H U K O K
— R I E — T I R E
— B E — S I N G I N G
C O N S I D E R — E L O N
O R E — N E B A T — A S A
L O W — G N A S H — H E W

PUZZLE 3

R T E — K I S H I — H O
A R A — O T H E R — J A M
S O — W H E E L — G A T E
H U P H A M — M A N N E R
— B O A T S — P A N
S L O T H — A T T A I N
E E R — I R S — C O
A S E N A T H — O W N E R
— R O B — A B I A
— T I — A N A N I A S
B R E E D I N G — D O S T
E A R — A R E L I — T I E
E W E — N A M E S — H A P

PUZZLE 4

— Q U A K E — T E A C H
S U P P E R — H A S H E M
H E — T E R R O R S — L O
E N — P E A R S — K I
D C C — T E N — W A S
S H E L A H — S P I R I T
— A I R — U S E
J A S P E R — E L A S A H
A T E — H A S — T H E
S A — H O S T S — I S
O R — G O D H E A D — M E
N A T U R E — E L I D A D
H O R N S — M A D O N

PUZZLE 5

```
S I A H A   A L O O F
C I T I E S   H A N N A H
A S   M E T   Y E   I E
L E A V E N E D     E R R
A R B A   A M A   E Y E D
H A I L   T A T T L E R S
    S U A H   E P I
E P H E R     H A B
A H A S A I   S O R E R
S U I T   T I T H E   T O
E R   B A S H A N   H E
D A N I E L   A G A B U S
  H O N E Y   N E I E L
```

PUZZLE 6

```
  H I N E S   H E A P S
B O T T L E   O W N E T H
O R   H A N D L E D   A I
A R   M A I D S   I R
R O M   A G E   A R A
D R I E T H   N A H A S H
    D R S   P A R
S E E D   S T R O K E
B A T   A H A   N O N
A M   S M O T E   H O
R I   S A N D A L S   A S
S T A L E   N A H A T H
S A L A D   S H E T H
```

PUZZLE 7

```
K I N G L Y   J A A K A N
I T   N E E D E T H   S O
S E A T   I S A I A H
  D T S   S I D O N
U Z   A H A   A S
S E P H A R   H A G A B A
E P H E R   T I D A L
S H I M M A   B E N O N I
T I   H A I   A M
    I S A   S T R A W
  S N U B   A T O N E S
O P   C L O S E S T   H E
G A T H E R   R E S T E D
```

PUZZLE 8

```
  H O N O R   S T E P S
B E N O N I   H O P E T H
U Z   R E S H E P H   A I
K I   S E A L S   R R
K O A   S I A   A R A
I N F A N T   H E R E S H
    O R O   R A N
R O O T E D   S I M O N S
A R T   R O E   N E H
H A   H O B A H   T O
A T   S O P A T E R   H E
B O W E L S   E R I T E S
R E A D Y   D E B I R
```

PUZZLE 9

```
  A M   V I S I T   A N
A R A N   O T H N I   H O
P A R A D I S E   W E T
O H   M I C   A C   A R E
  D E M E T R I U S
O N E   S O   E R   S A
B E N O   O L I V E S
A R   I S   S N   O A K
  S L I M E   P A W S
R I E   A I   E Z   O F
I R A   N A H A M A N I
B I T H Y N I A   O M E R
  S E E I N G   N E D
```

PUZZLE 10

```
  S O L E S   O Z I A S
K O H A T H   N E R I A H
E D   M A A S I A I   P E
N O   M A H O L   H E
A M I   P E N   O I L
N A M E T H   S T A I R S
    N A H   O W L
S E A R E D   S P E E C H
A S H   E S T   D O E
T H   F A I R S   O R
A T   D A L A I A H   L O
N O T I C E   F L O W E D
N I G E R   E A R E D
```

PUZZLE 11

```
    H O     U R I E L
J O N A   N I S R O C H
E M E R A L D S     L O T
W E   A R E   U S   A S H
      C H A S T E N E D
K I R     S O   O H   H A
A M Y L       S W I P E S
F P     I A   D A     O A K
      J E R A H   E B E R
A H A   M M   P E   D O
S U R   E I G H T E E N
P R E T E N S E     A L S O
      B I D D E N     H I T
```

PUZZLE 12

```
          A L B S
        E X C E E D
      A R E   S A I D
    D U E   A T T I R E
A E R   E N O S     E A T
S P A R R O W   S A R A H
I E   E I N   F P M   L I
A N G L E   T R U S T E D
  D E I   H E E D   O N E
    R E P E N T   A R T
      D E A D   I A N
        T R E N C H
          T R E E
```

PUZZLE 13

```
        I R A S
      T E M P T S
    W A R   P A C O
  V I N   V E R I L Y
W O N   K I A S   I E R
E T E R N A L   A V A I L
A I   E E L   O N E   D A
K N I F E   A N O T H E R
  G T O   I R A N   A R K
    O R I S O N   A L S
      M A S U   H G T
        L U N G E R
          E D O M
```

PUZZLE 14

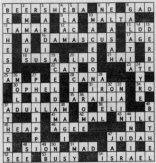

```
B E E R S H E B A   N E   G A D
E   M A   L A   M A L T A
T A M A R   A C A A     L O D
H A   D A M A S C U S     A G E
E   U I       E A T     R
S   S U S A   L I D   H A I
D       C A Y   O     A T E
A M P E     C A N A       Y
O P H E L   I   I R O N   R O
  L I D   A R A B I A     A
A D U L L A M   O E L I
T   I   M A   M A L   N I L E
H E A P   A G E E     N   T
E     P I       J U D A H
N   S I O N   M A D   A I E
S E E   B U S Y   I S R A E L
```

PUZZLE 15

```
M I R A C L E   A R K     M
I   A C H A R   B E   V A
N   H U B   A B A S E
I C H A B O D   A C H I M
S   A I   U E   H A N D
T A L C   R E S T   V
E   L U Z   R I V E R S
R   O S E E   O R P H A N
  S W   L L A M A     C A
S H E L O M I   S O   H I
    E D I T   R I   T E L
A M   V E X   O P H E L
S   R E S I D U E     N
```

PUZZLE 16

```
S T A R     B U Y S   M A
H O P E   D E P O T   L
A P P L E   T O U R
R   L I P S   N   I T I S
  Y E A H       P O L E
E N   D   A B E L   M I T
N E T   M O N E Y     E
  S H A D E   O N E   S T
S T O R Y   J U D A H   H
A   R O E   E G   R I P E
T U N E D   S H E L T E R
A S   R   B U   C Y C L E
N A Y   P E S T O   H T
```

PUZZLE 17

PUZZLE 18

PUZZLE 19

PUZZLE 20

PUZZLE 21

PUZZLE 22

PUZZLE 23

S	O	B			P	I	P	E			S	W	A	T
O	R	A			A	T	E	R			P	A	V	E
P	E	R			R	E	A	R			E	R	I	E
		N	O	A	M			A	M	E	N	D	S	
S	T	A	I	D			E	N	I	D				
T	A	B	L	E			A	D	D			G	O	A
A	L	A	S			I	T	S			S	L	I	P
Y	E	S			N	N	E			H	E	E	L	S
			J	O	H	N			E	R	A	S	E	
A	D	H	E	R	E			K	E	E	N			
M	I	A	S			R	A	I	D			I	R	E
E	C	R	U			I	D	L	E			N	O	N
N	E	T	S			T	E	N	D			G	O	D

PUZZLE 24

C	A			S	E	B	A			S	H	A	M	E
U	R			S	T	E	M			L	I	N	E	N
R	E	S			A	T			W	O	R	D		
B	A	T	T	L	E			A	W	E			A	I
S		A	R			A	S			S	A	N	D	
		R	E	T	E	S	T				T	H	E	E
T	E			O	N	S	E	T				M	A	
O	B	E	D			M	E	D	I	U	M			
M	E	N	E				I	S			S	O	R	T
E	D			S	A	T			D	E	E	P	E	R
		T	I	N	Y			R	A			S	P	A
S	H	A	R	E			H	O	R	N			A	D
S	T	R	E	W			A	P	S	E			Y	E

PUZZLE 25

D	A	M			H	O	R	S	E			B	I	D
O	B	E	Y			G	A	L	L			U	T	E
M	E	L	E	E			H	A	Z	E	R	I	M	
			T	A	L	L			Y	A	R	N	S	
G	R	I	S	L	E	D			B	A	T			
R	A	N	T			A	R	B	A	S			B	Y
E	G	G			A	V	O	I	D			B	E	E
W	E			C	R	E	W	S			B	L	E	W
		M	A	R			N	O	T	I	O	N	S	
D	A	V	I	D				N	E	T	S			
F	O	R	E	V	E	R			N	E	S	T	S	
E	R	R			E	B	E	R			S	O	R	E
W	A	Y			S	T	O	W	S			M	A	T

PUZZLE 26

B	A	R	A	K			H	A	G	G	I	A	H
L		O	D	E	S			S	E	E	T	H	E
A	H			D	E	E	P			M	E		E	A
R	I	M			P	L	O	W	S			F	A	R
E	N	O	S			A	T	E			D	A	R	K
		D	A	T	A			E			H	I		T	E
C			B	E	G	I	N	N	I	N	G			N
O	H			R	E			T			S	E	R	F
N	O	O	N			P	A	W			D	O	E	R
C	R	Y			C	I	T	E	S			W	E	E
E	N			G	O			E	S	A	U			T	I
D	E	S	E	R	T			T	U	R	N			N
E	T	E	R	N	A	L			L	I	O	N	S

PUZZLE 27

R	E	P			A	B	E	A	M			S	T	A
O	E	R			S	E	R	V	E			P	A	W
B	R	O	T	H	E	R			S	P	I	N	E	
			P	E	E	P			T	S	A	R			
G	A	H	A	R			F	A	I	R	E	S	T	
A	H	E	M			G	E	R	A			T	O	
A	L	T			E	L	I	A	S			J	A	W
S	A			T	O	S	H			T	U	R	N	
H	I	G	H	E	S	T			N	E	S	T	S	
			H	E	R	S			G	O	A	T			
S	T	E	R	N			S	O	R	R	O	W	S	
E	O	N			A	N	I	A	M			N	O	E
W	E	T			L	O	R	D	S			E	N	E

PUZZLE 28

E	T	C	H			T	I	S			O	B	O	E
N	R	A			P	A	S	T	E			A	L	L
D	I	S	T	A	L			U	G	A	N	D	A	
		C	H	A	L	C	E	D	O	N	Y			M
K	E	N			N					T	A	P		
A	S	S			A	G	A	T	E			N	A	G
I	T			D	I	A	M	O	N	D			N	O
M	E	N			D	R	E	G	S			B	A	G
R	I	O			L					L	A	T		
N			C	H	R	Y	S	O	L	Y	T	E		
A	T	E	M	P	O			P	U	E	B	L	O	
N	I	L			H	Y	R	A	X			O	A	R
O	N	Y	X			O	I	L			L	Y	S	E

PUZZLE 29

```
S H Y   D A S H     S P O T
L E E   A C H E     N O A H
I A   D I N E     D A I R Y
P R A I S E     H I P S
    W R Y     B E S P E A K
S U E T     M E R C Y     S I
O L D     B A A L S     G I N
A N   V E N U S     B R A D
P A T I E N T     G E E
    O R C A     P R A Y E R
F A I T H     C A E N     D O
L U L U     L O V E     W E D
T O E     O P E N     O N E
```

PUZZLE 30

```
S U S A     C R A B     R U N
S P E D     Z O B A     O N E
E S A U     A B E L     A D O
    L O R E     A A R O N
A M I T Y       S A X
J E R   S A L E M     M I O
A D A M   B I T     B O T H
R E N   B E T H L E H E M
      O U T       A T O M S
C H U R N       S A S H
H A G   D E E P     A C T S
I L L   L O N E     N O A H
P L Y   E N D S     Y O R E
```

PUZZLE 31

```
R E A M   C O W     H O P E
I D D O   O R O     E N O S
D E A R   R A N     W E R E
      T I P     D I E
L A B A N S     E N R A G E
S T E R N E     R E S C U E
    R A             H A
R I S E U P   T E M A N S
N A T U R E     A R E N O T
      R U N     B E D
U N D O   U A R     D O R A
R E A P   R T E     L E A H
I R M A   Y E T     E R M A
```

PUZZLE 32

```
B A N C   F I R     E B E D
B R I O   U R E     L O V E
B O N N   R A N     E D E N
  N E C R O M A N C E R
        E A R     M O T
L I M I T   F E D     W O N
E R A T   R E D   V I N E
T A R   H E M     F I N E R
      S E M     S I N
  A S T R O L O G E R S
A S E A   V A N     G O A D
T I L L   E R G     A D I N
T A L L   D D S     R E L A
```

PUZZLE 33

```
        C A B S
    S A M E C H
  G I N   W H I T
  M O N   P A I N E D
S O N   W A R N   M E R
P R E S A G E   S P O I L
I T   T I E   S H E   V I
N A B A L   C H A R G E R
  L E V   C H O W   E R A
    N E P H E E   P E S
      E P E E   A I R
          D E S E R T
            R E N T
```

PUZZLE 34

```
A R I A   D E B     A C R E
S E L F   U R E     T R U E
A G E E   R A H     T Y N E
      A P E     A R E
T A R S U S     V A N I T Y
A R E T A S     E N D U R E
M I S             A A
E S T E E M     R E N O I R
R E S C U E     A L I E N S
      C R T     C I S
A B E L   H A H     A N N A
W E R E   E R E     N E A R
E A R S   G A L     S E E M
```

PUZZLE 35

```
A L A S | | P P D | | N O A H
S A R A | A L E | | A N T I
A M A T | O S | | B A T S
| P H I L I P P I A N S |
| | S O D | A L L | |
S W I F T | M I L | | A R I
M A N Y | B A R | A S I A
U S E | A R T | K N E E L
| | P S I | S E A | |
| I N H A B I T A N T S |
D E O | E R A | I O T A
L O R N | R A Y | A L A N
A L O E | Y E S | S A Y S
```

PUZZLE 36

```
A C T | S E T | | P E N
S A H | L A O | | E L A N
P R E D E S T I N A T E
S T R I P E | | S O T
| E N T | S O L O M O N
C A F E | P A L S | O L E
A G O D | L U D | A R E A
M A R | G A T E | S T O P
P R E S A G E | S E A
| L I I | S E A L E D
P R I N C I P A L I T Y
A I D S | | S A T | T R E
N A E | | M T S | Y E S
```

PUZZLE 37

```
A N E W | A S P | N E T S
T E R I | M I L | E L O I
T E E D | E R A | P I R N
| O W N | N I H |
S H E W E D | K E E P E R
C O A S T S | S O W E T H
O R G | | | T H E
R E L I E D | A E N E A S
E M E R G E | S M Y R N A
| E O N | S E M |
M U N | I R E | P Y R E
A R B A | E A R | H A I R
D I S H | D E T | M E N
```

PUZZLE 38

```
T A P | A R A M | S A S E
E S A | L A T U | I G O R
R I T | T I E R | N O N E
M A R V E L | | M E A
| I E R | J U N I P E R
S E A T | T A R O | R A E
E R R | S A K E S | O S E
L A C | A X E D | U S E D
A T H A I A H | A N E
| A L T | G U I L T Y
E B E R | I B A R | Y E A
V E T O | O O L A | T A R
E D E N | N O E L | E R N
```

PUZZLE 39

```
E T C | L A I C | S A M E
B A L | A N N O | T R U E
E R E | B O O N | R I D E
R E A S O N | | S I A
| N E R | B U L W A R K
E R | T | F A M E | B E E
R A W | S O R E S | U N E
A M A | A R E S | K N O P
S A Y I N G S | B I D
| M D I | M E R A R I
A S I A | V E E R | N O D
F L A G | E P E E | C O D
T Y N E | N I T A | E T O
```

PUZZLE 40

```
G S A | | S T A | P A I N
L A S T | Y E N | A B L E
I D E A | R E O | I B E X
B A R B | I N T E R E S T
| I R A | | H R |
T E N T H | J E S U R U N
A D A H | O R | N Y R O
J O N A D A B | S C E N T
| O T | | P O T |
T O G E T H E R | I S N T
A L I A | E P I | O C E
L I E S | N E Z | N O B S
C O R E | S E E | W O E
```

PUZZLE 41

```
A L L   C O A L   B A J A
W O E   O N C E   O N A M
E S T A T E   B E S I D E
      L E S T   N O M E
D O D O S   R O O M
E V E N   B A N C   L A D
B E N E A R   T H R O N E
T R Y   M A N O   A S T A
      S A Y S   E N T E R
T E M A N   C O C K
A R E T A S   B O S S E S
L A L A   A B E L   I R A
E N N   N   M E D E   R E D
```

PUZZLE 42

```
C A D   D O R   I R A D
A R I B   E V E   M O L E
P E A U   M U M   R U I N
T A L L   A M O R I T E S
        W A S   V E
W O M A N   H A V I L A H
E D A R   O I L   M E D E
S A C K B U T   L A V E R
        E T   S A G
C A S T A W A Y   I V A N
O M E R   A I R   N E B O
M E N U   R O I   E R L E
A N T E   D E A   Y E S
```